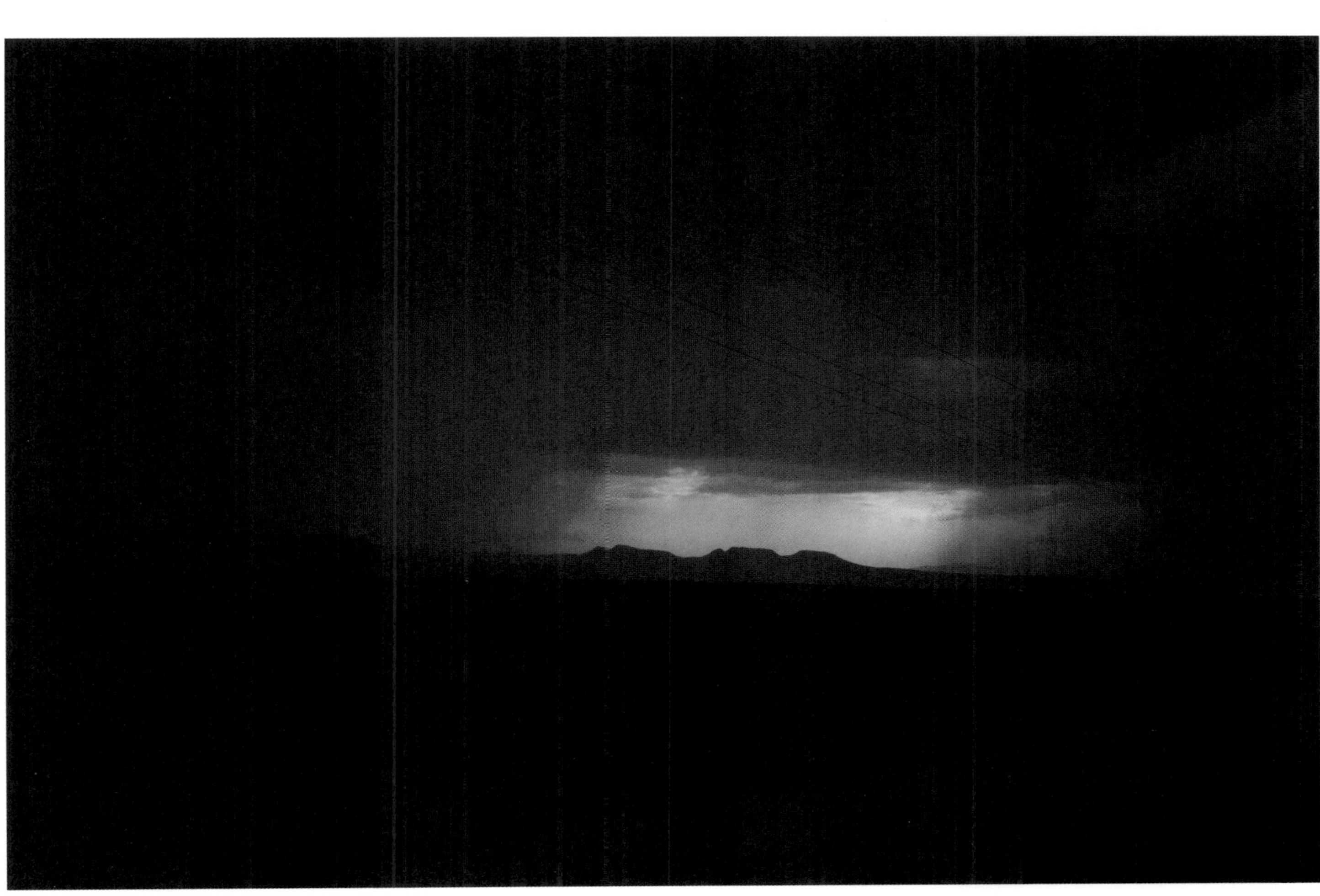

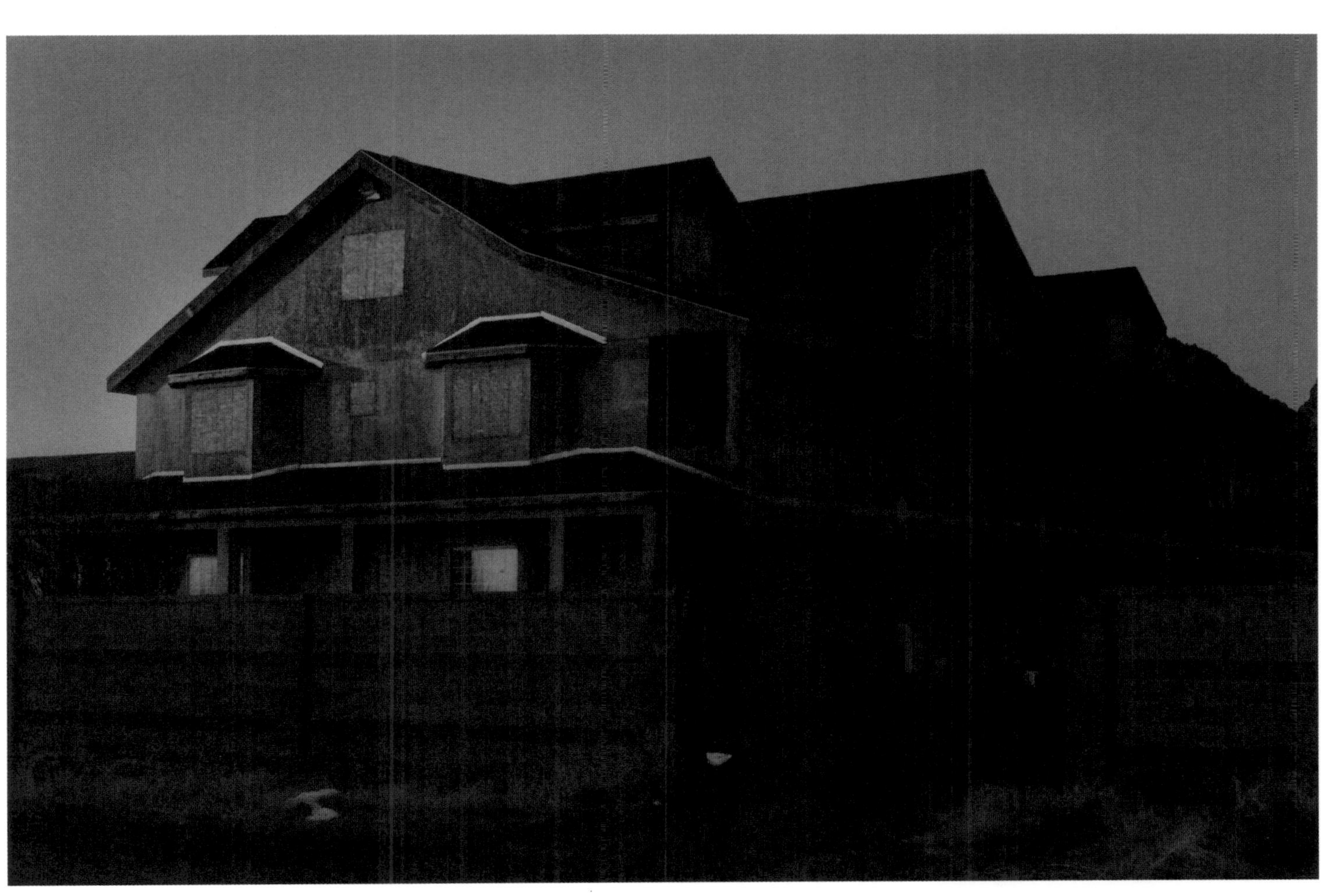

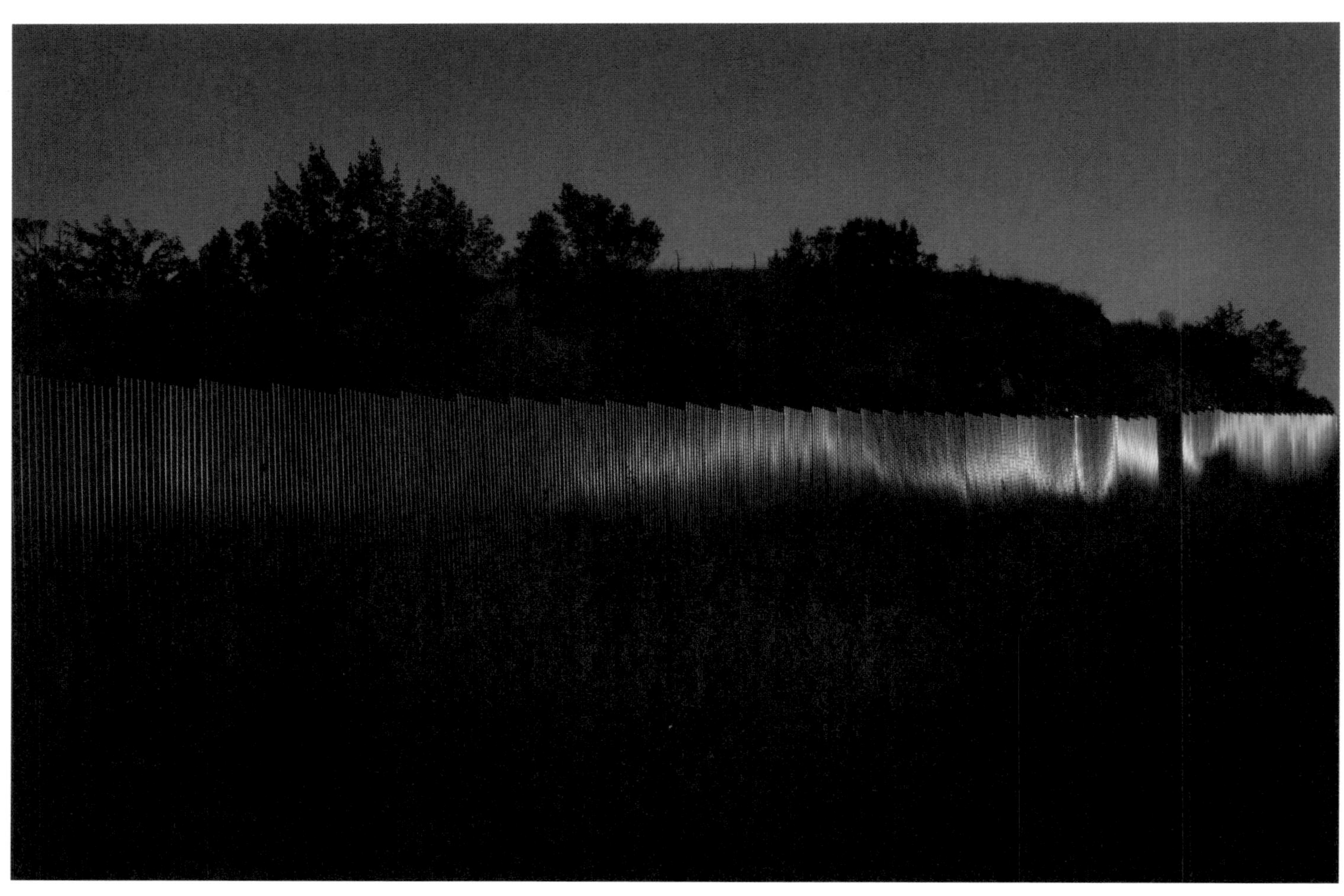

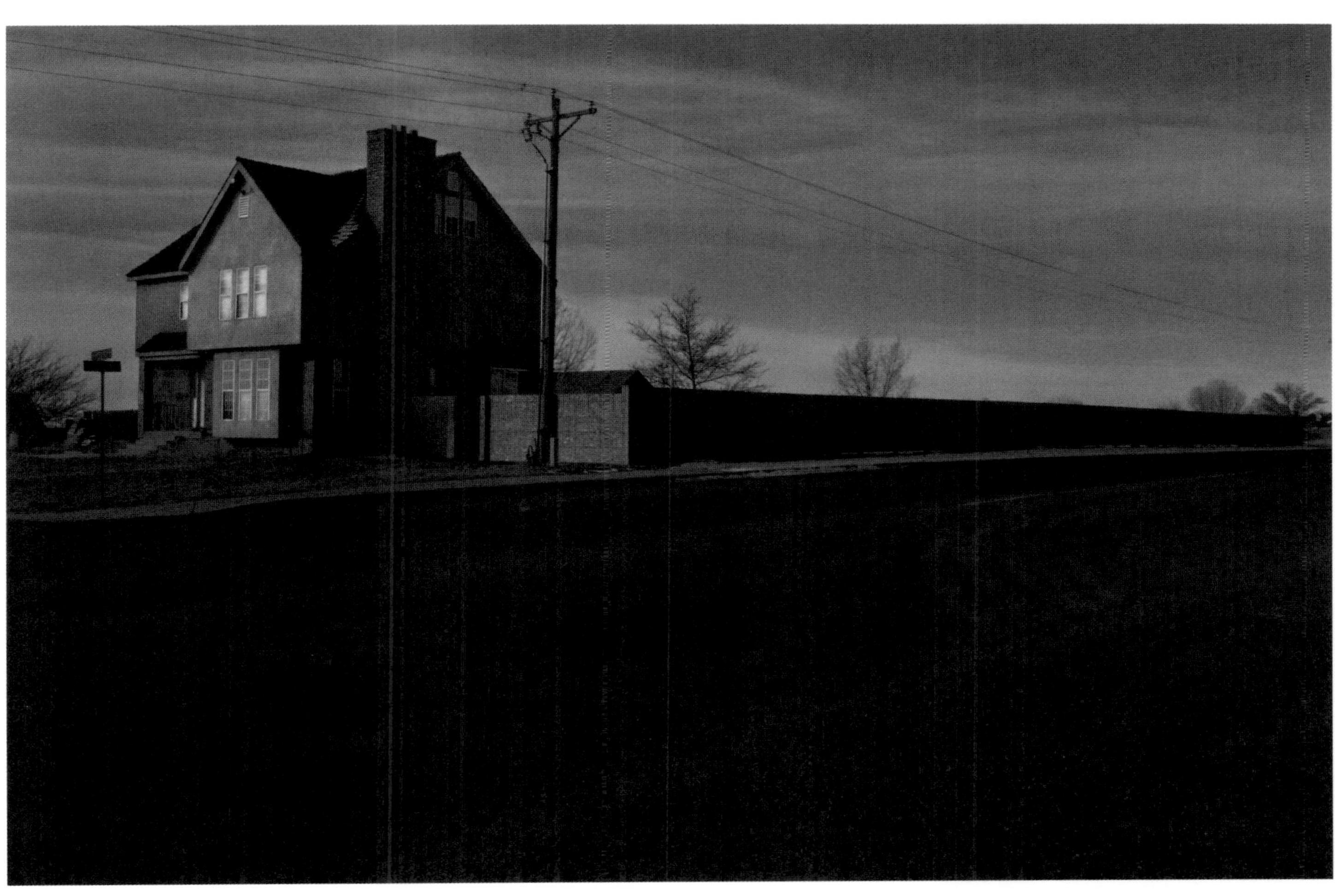

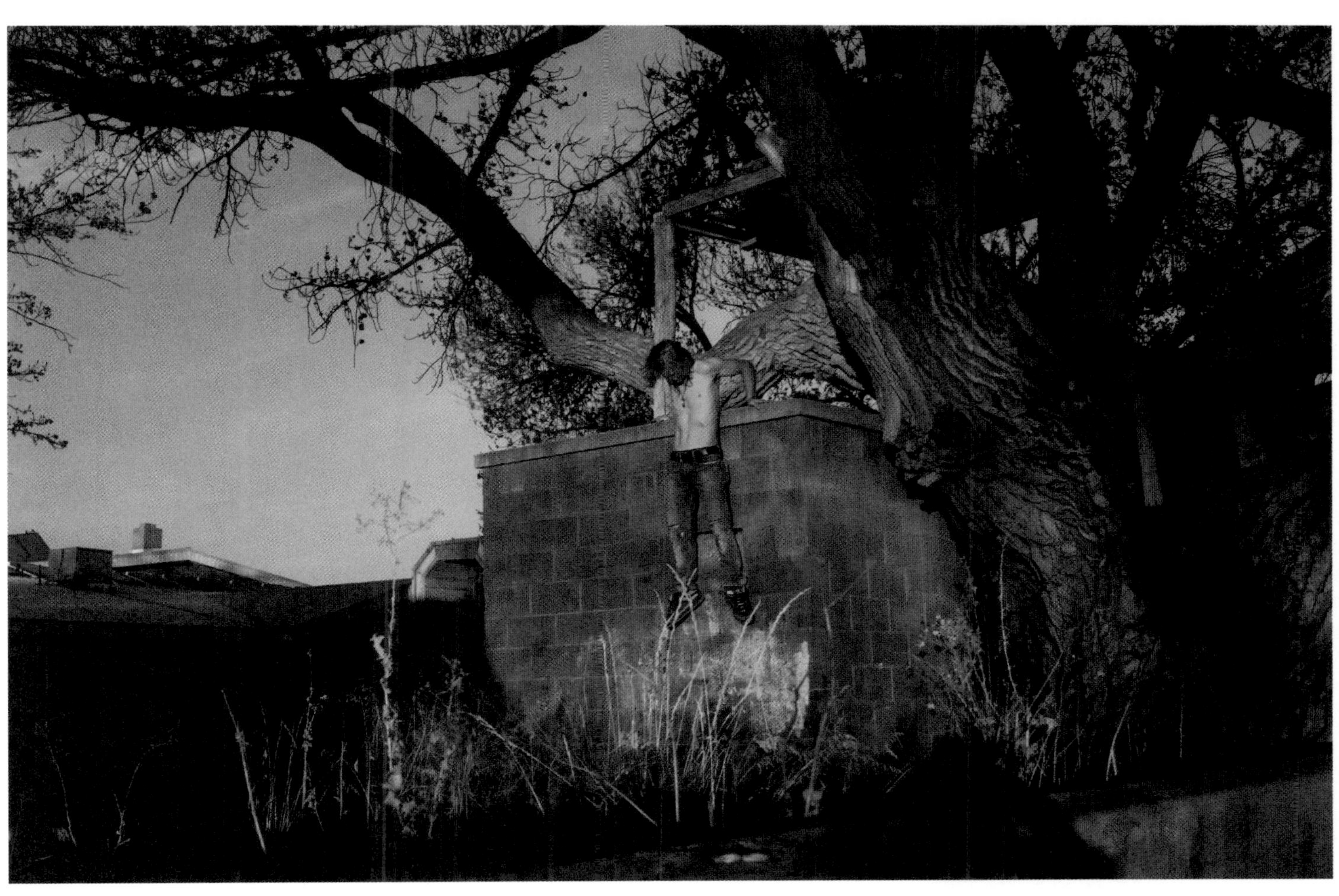

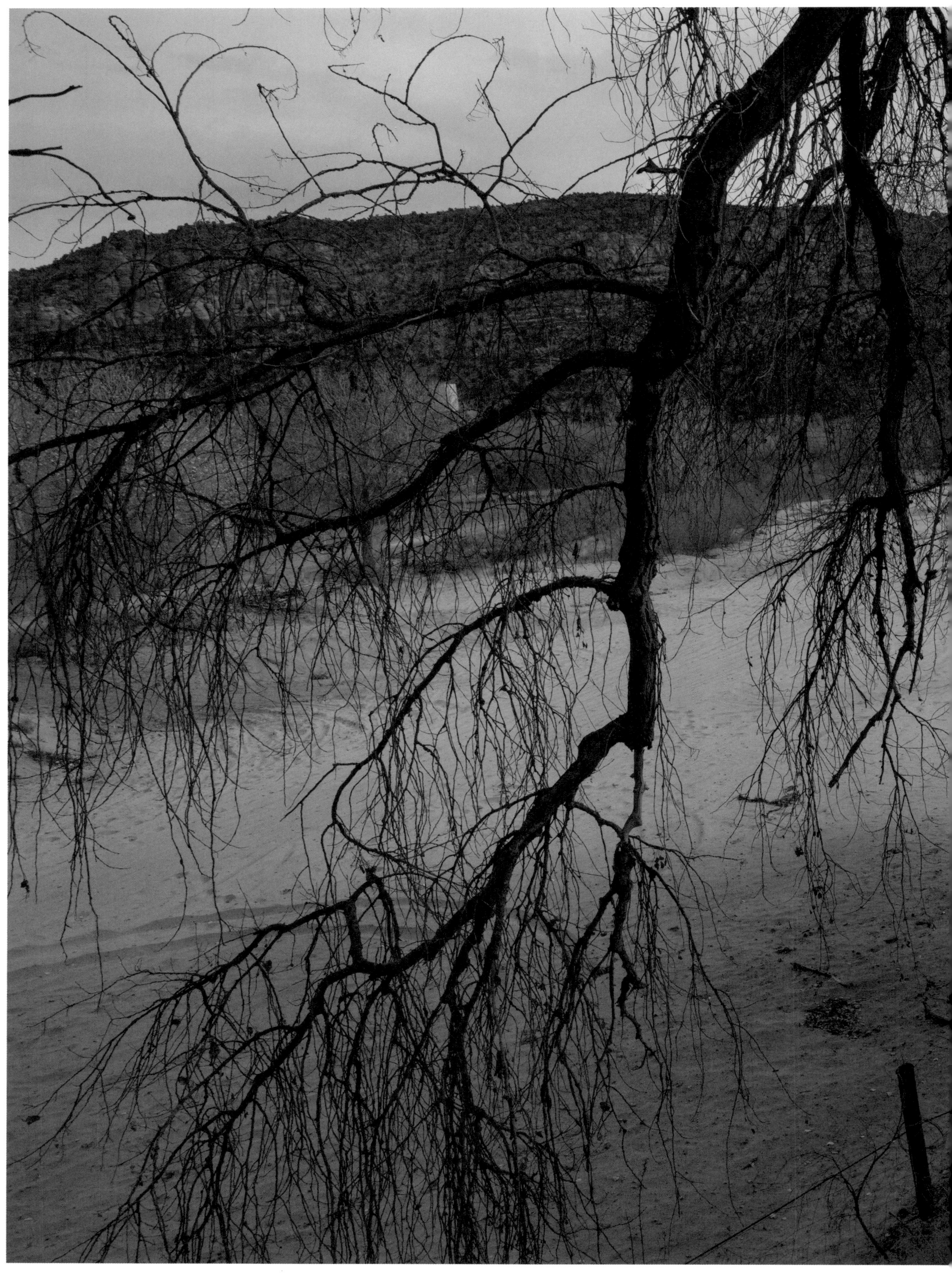

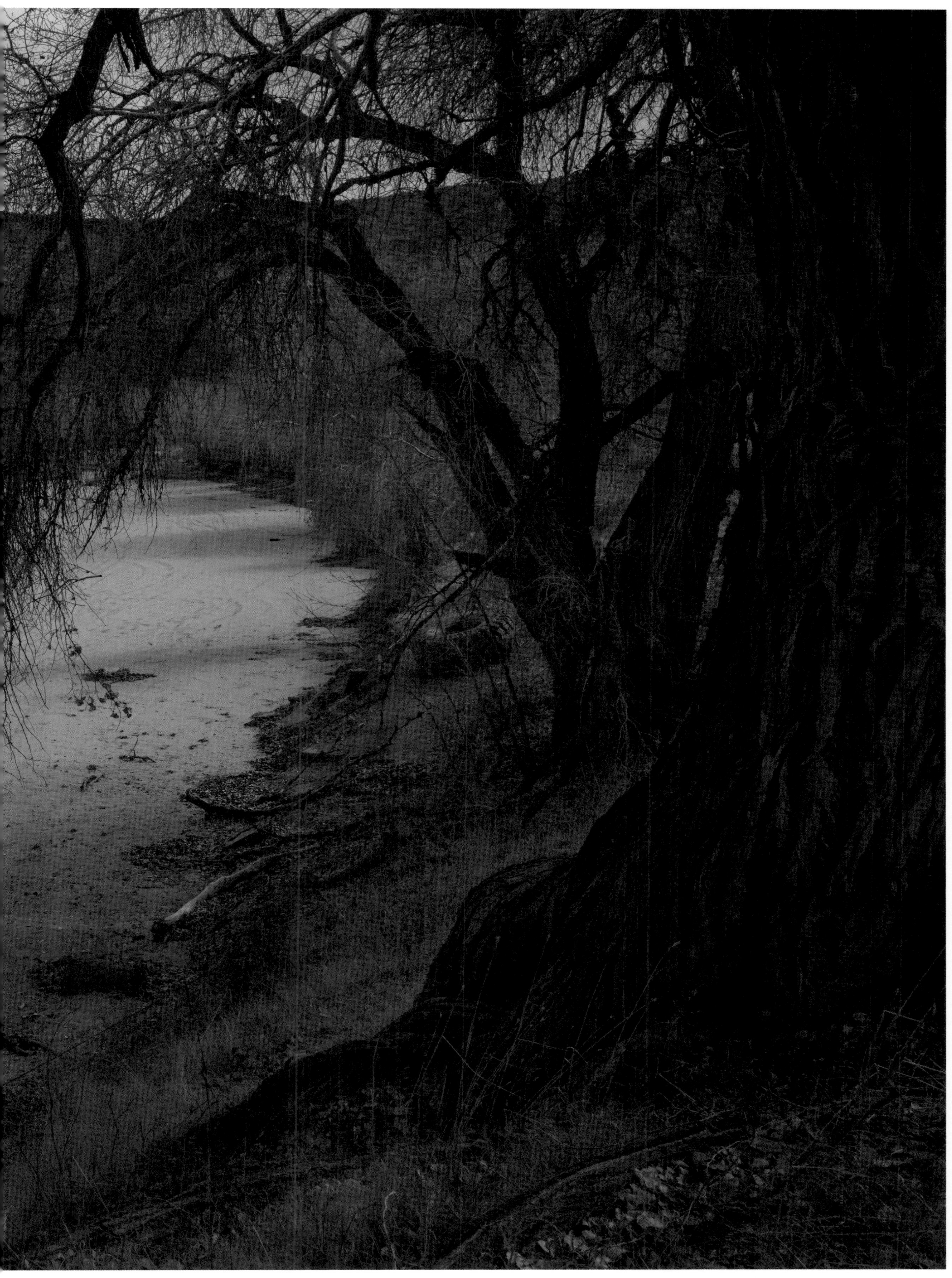

THE CRICK

Jim Mangan

TEXT
Judith Freeman

~

PROSE
Roman Bateman

TWIN PALMS PUBLISHERS

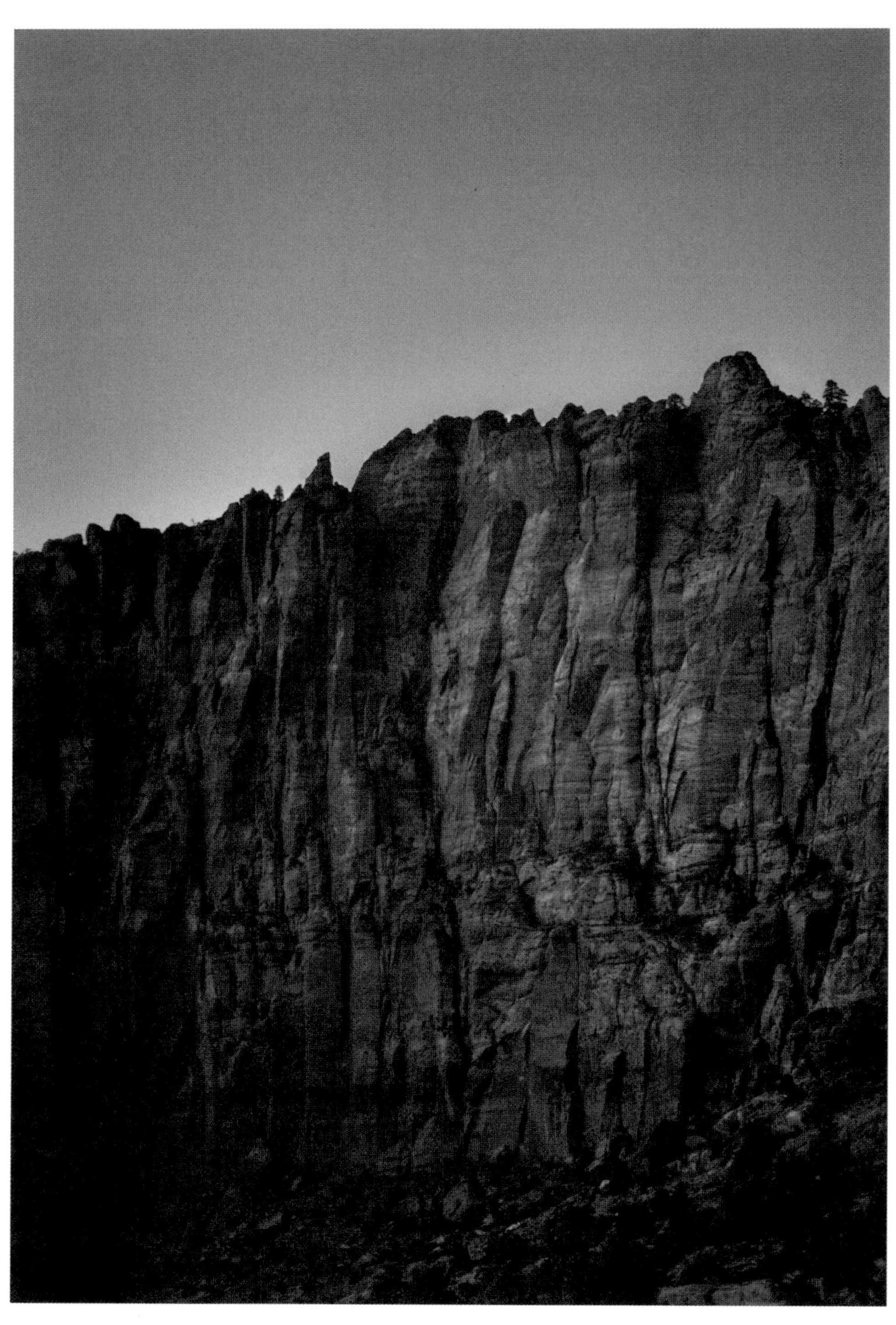

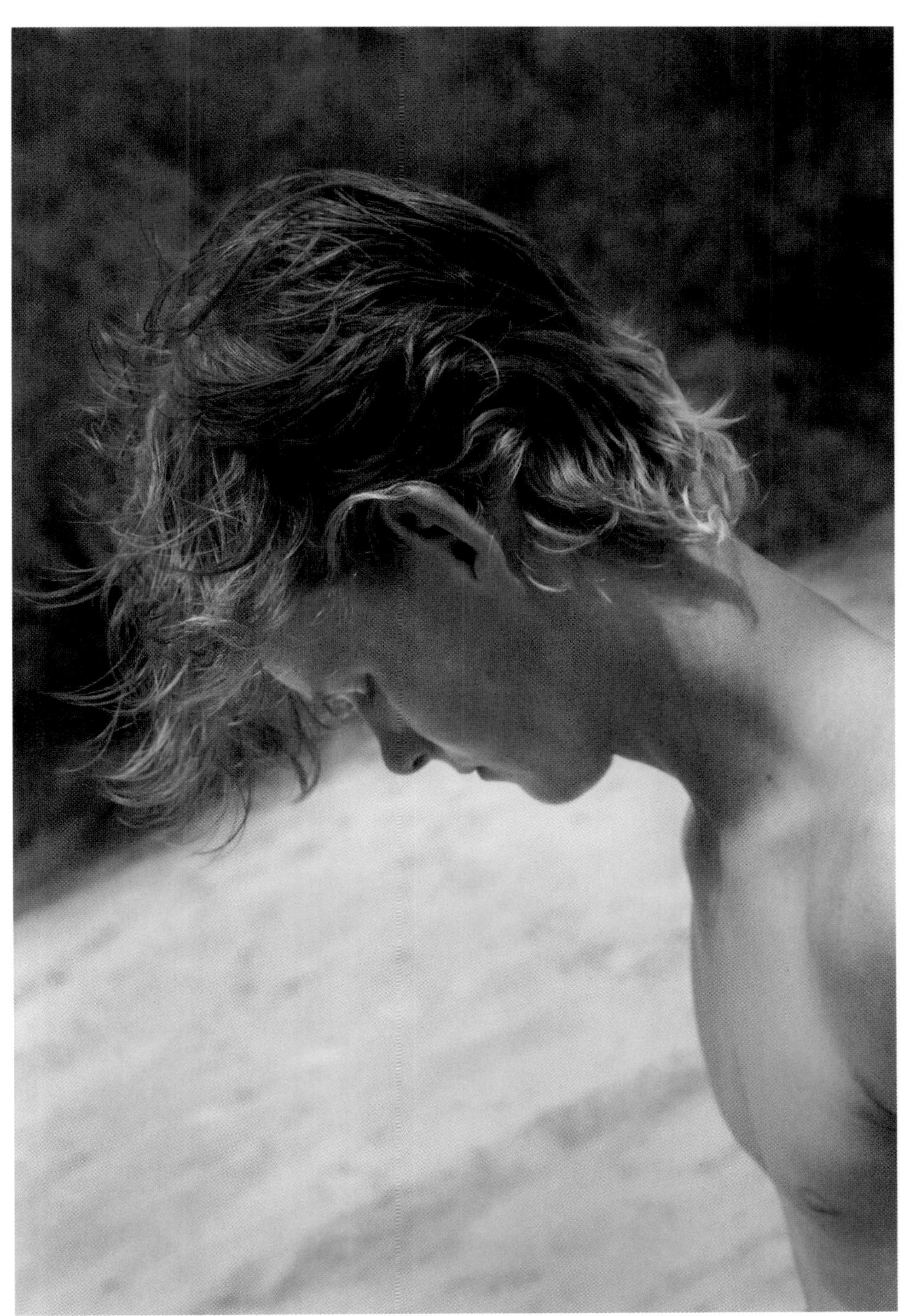

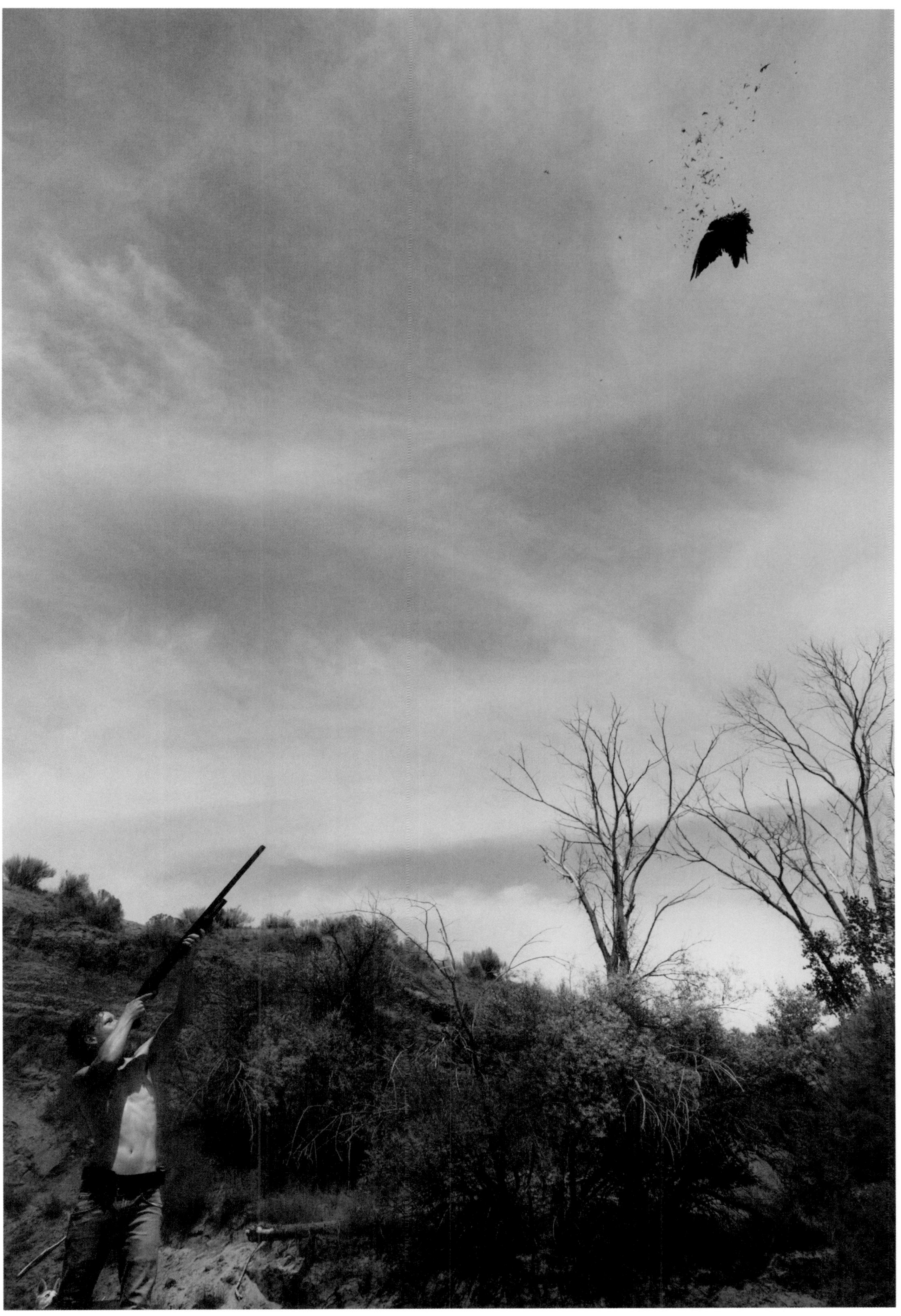

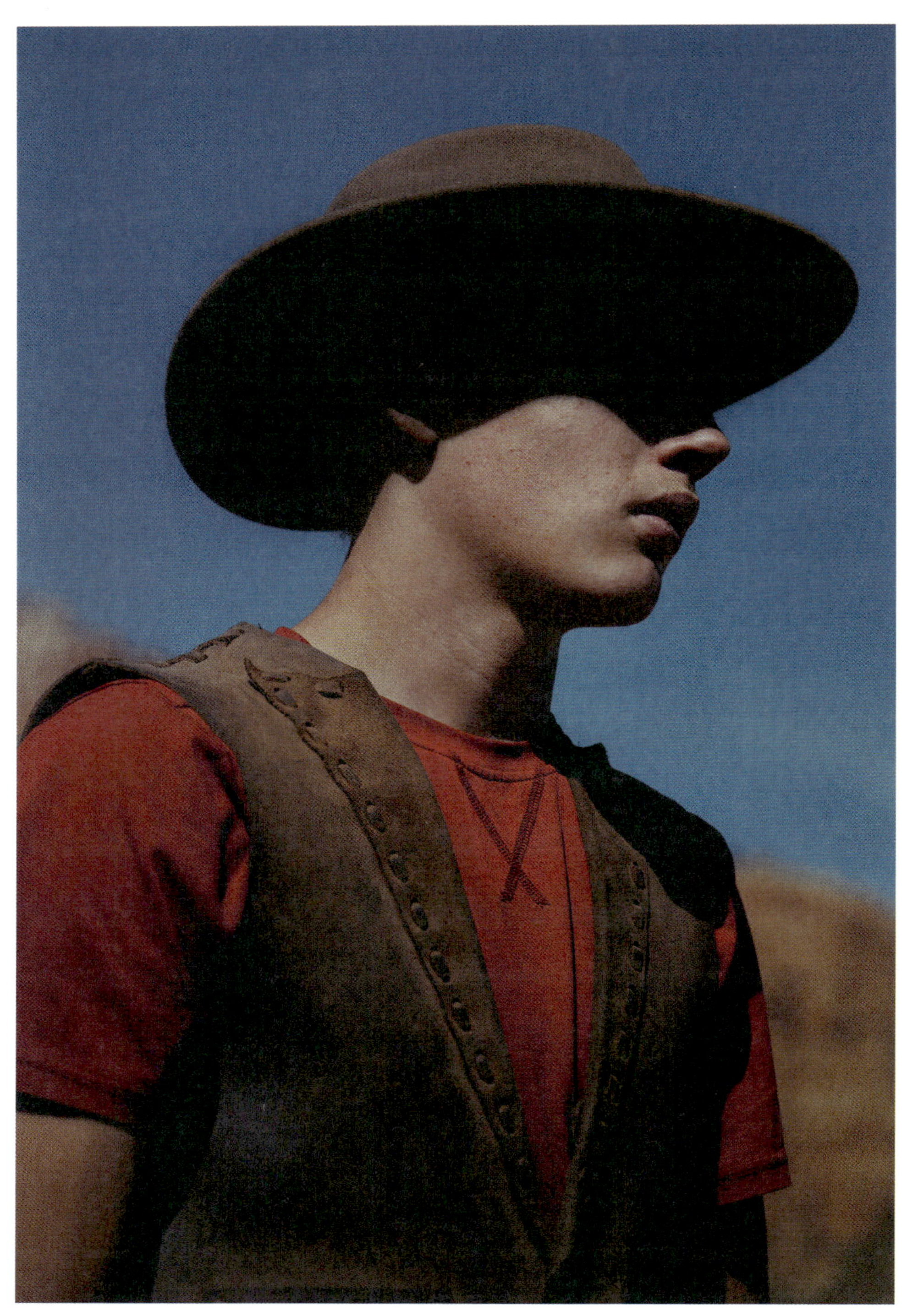

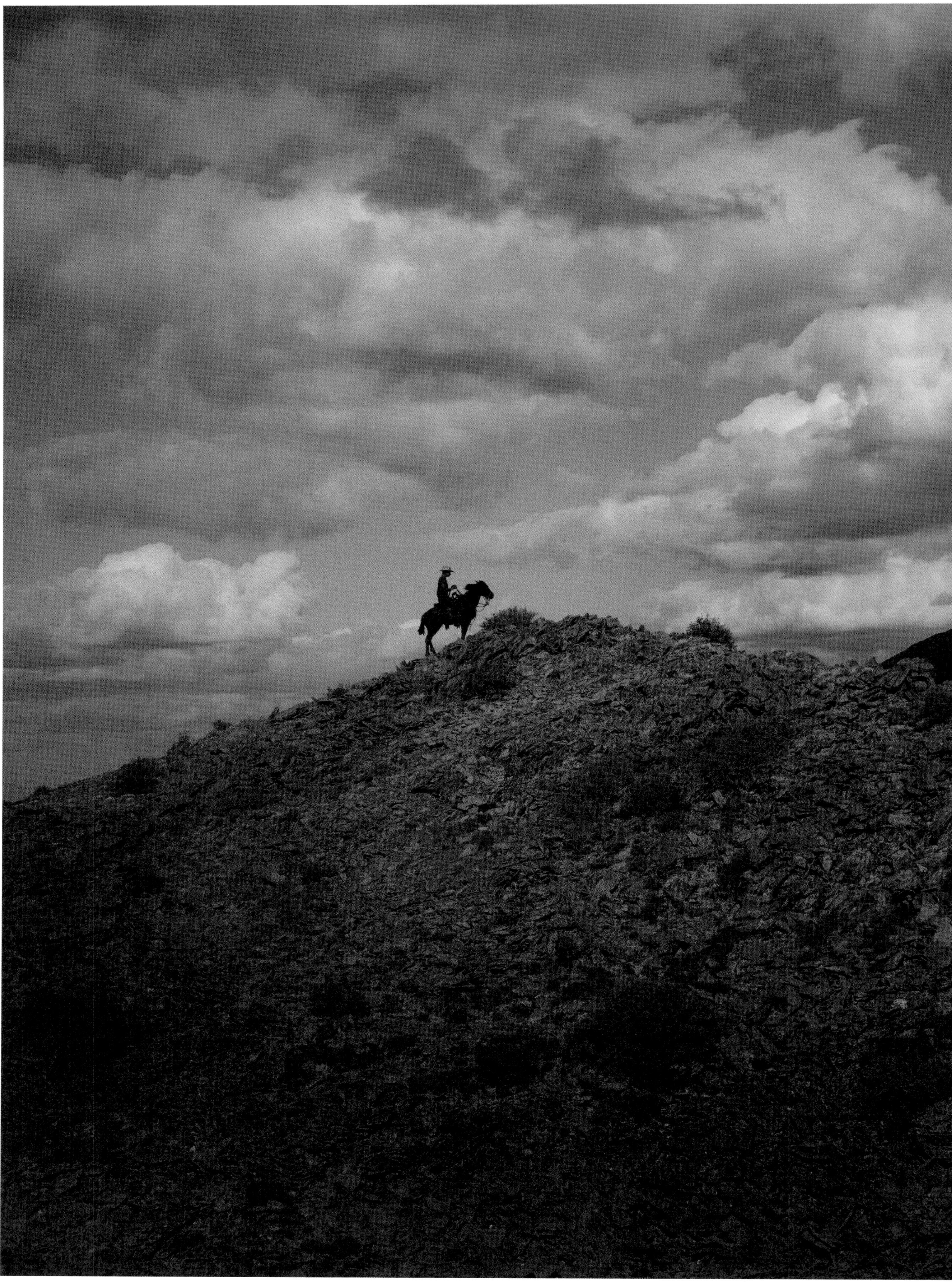

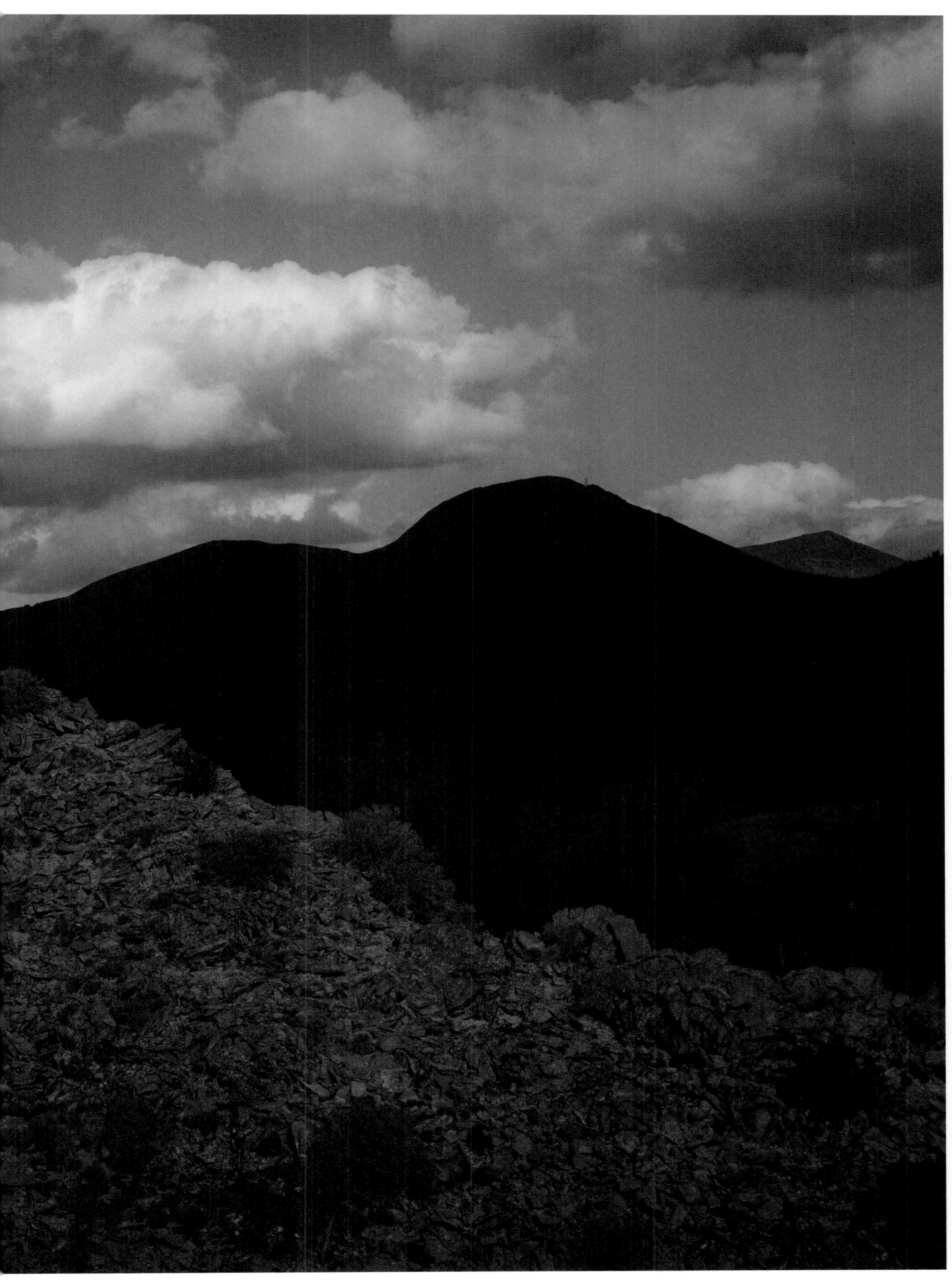

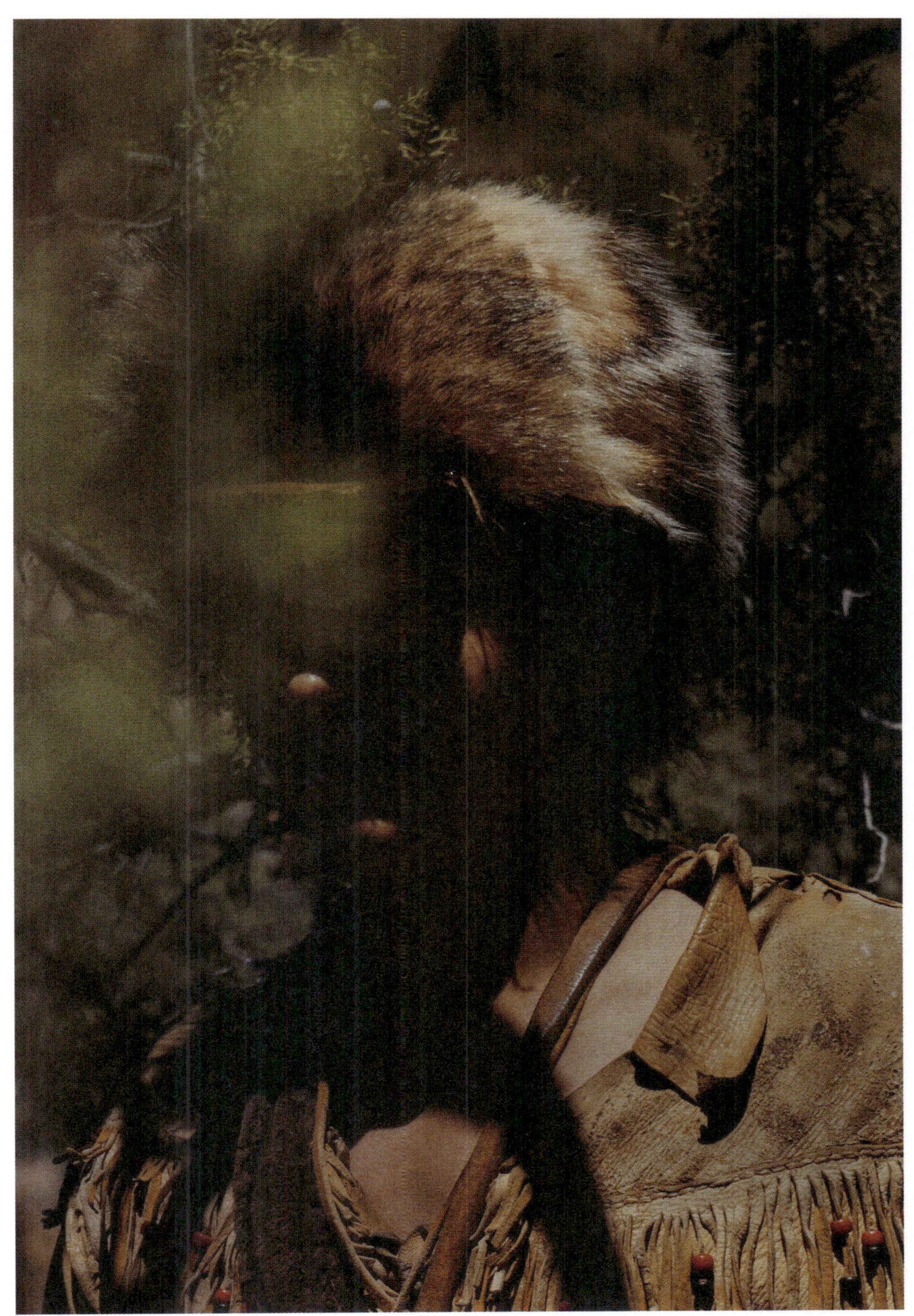

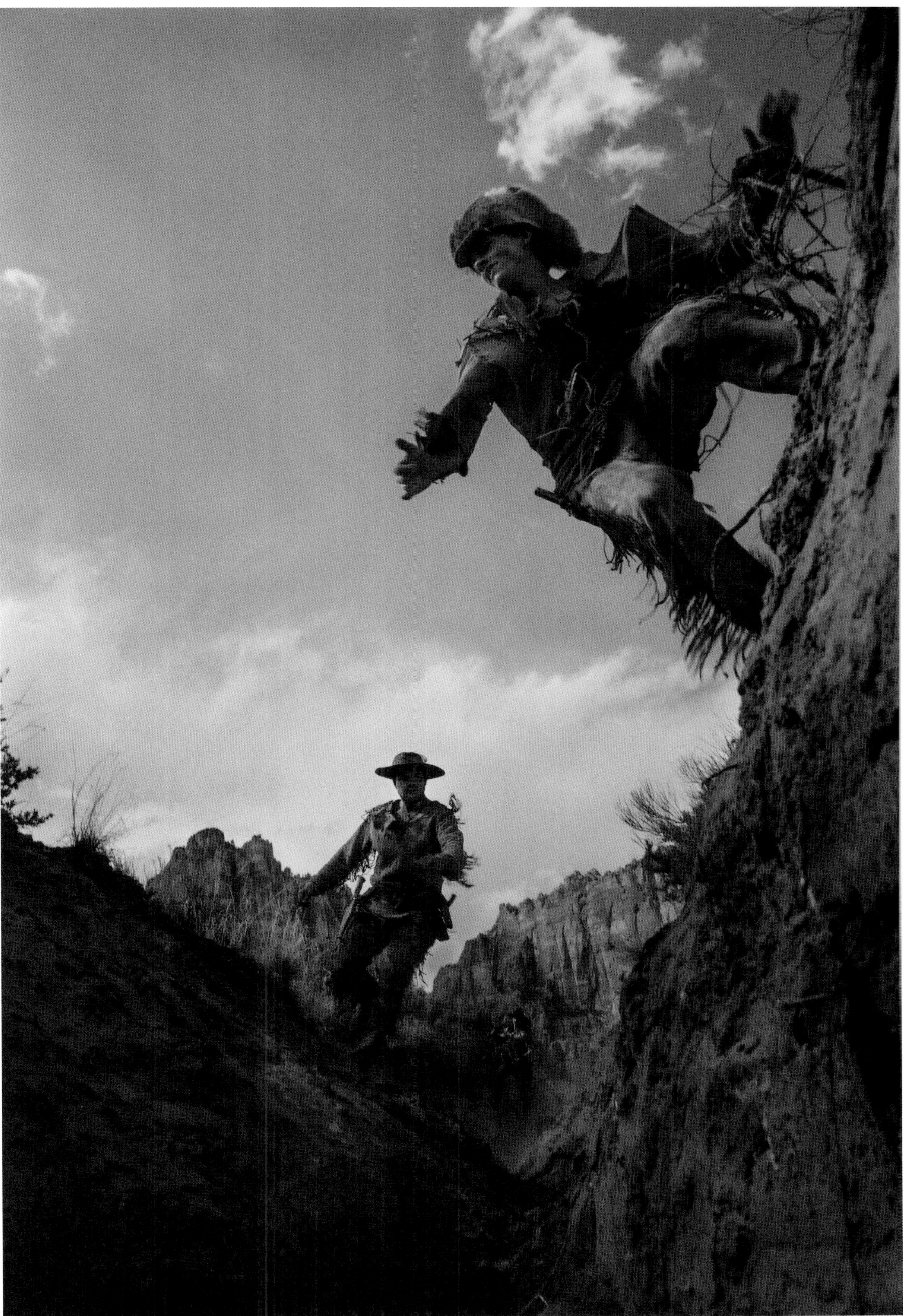

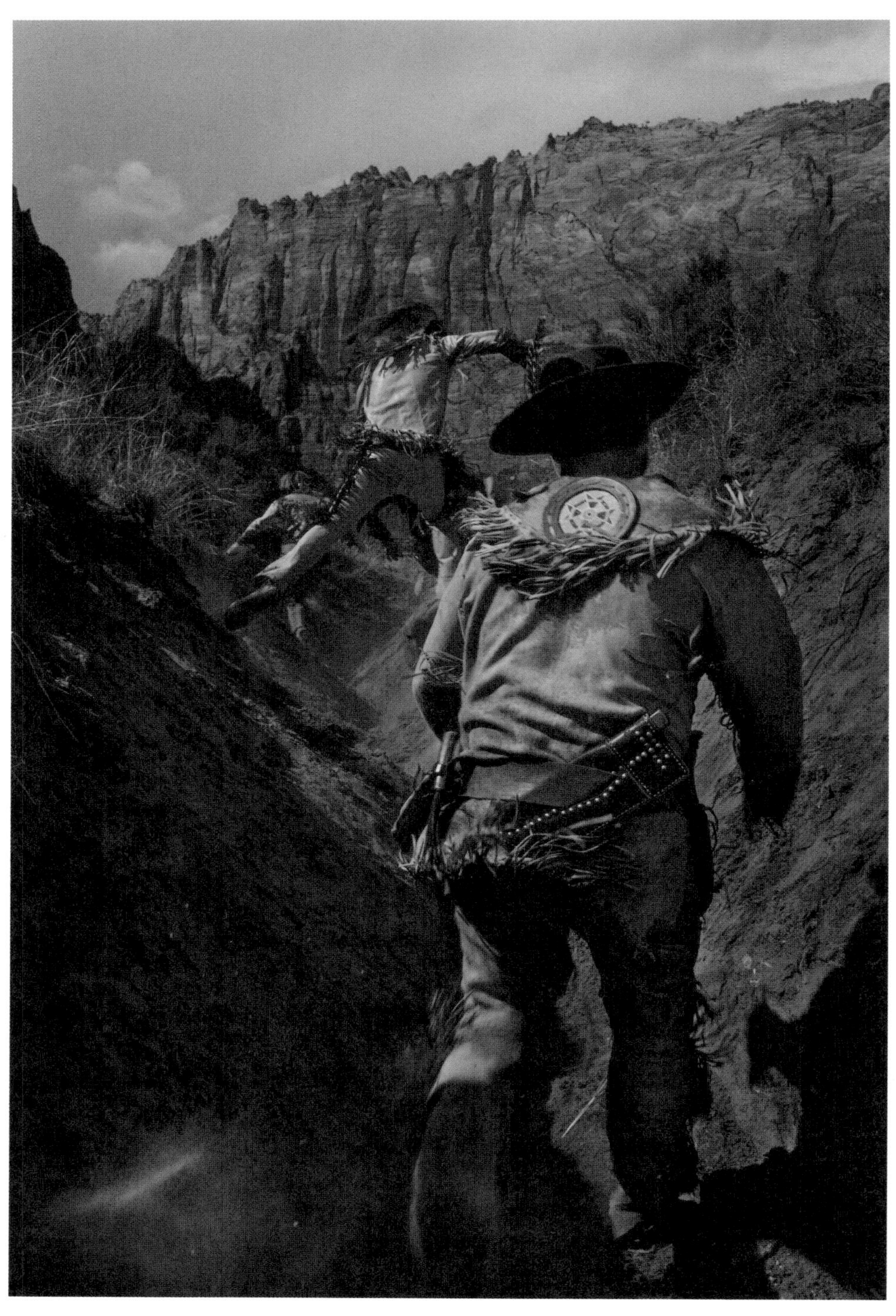

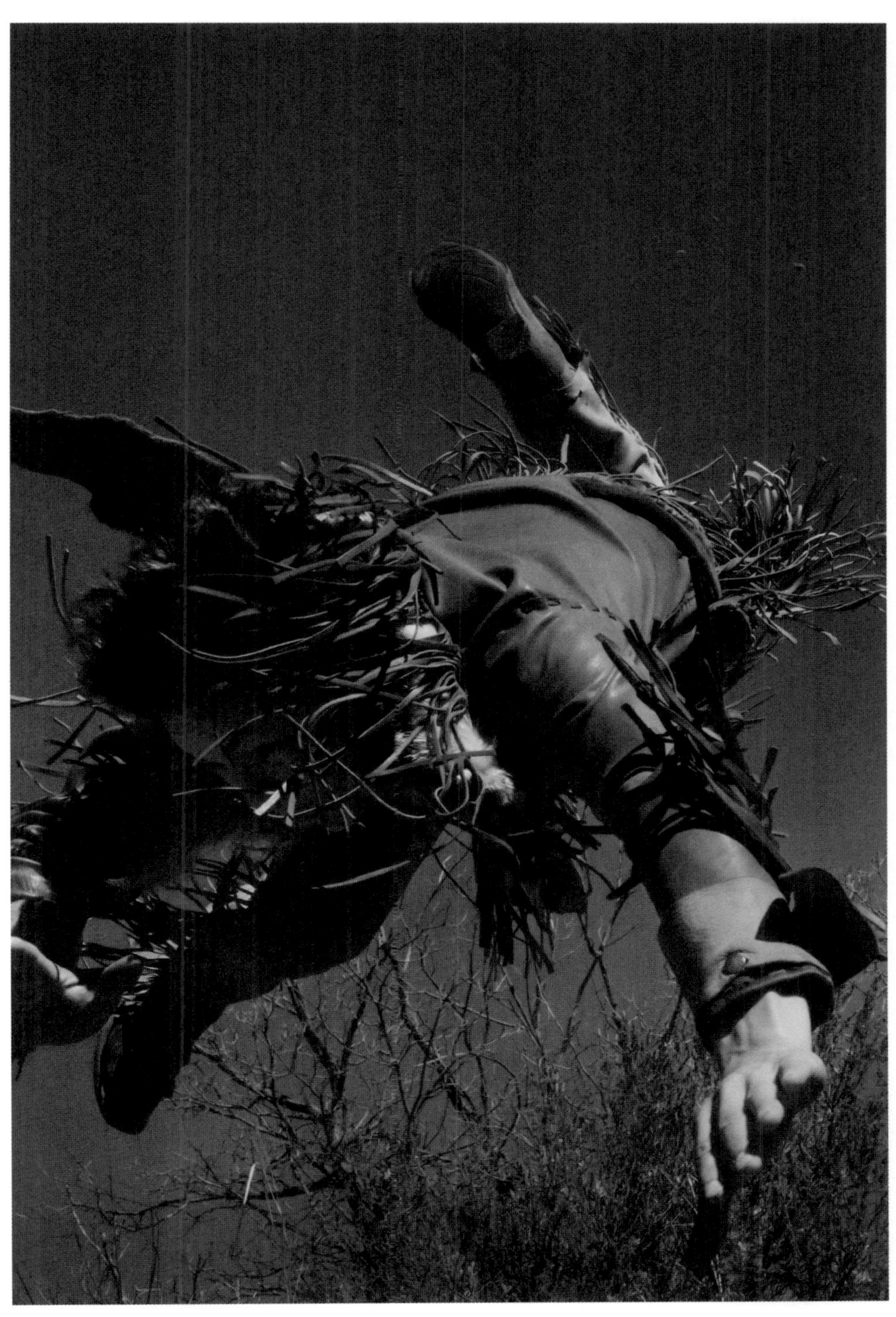

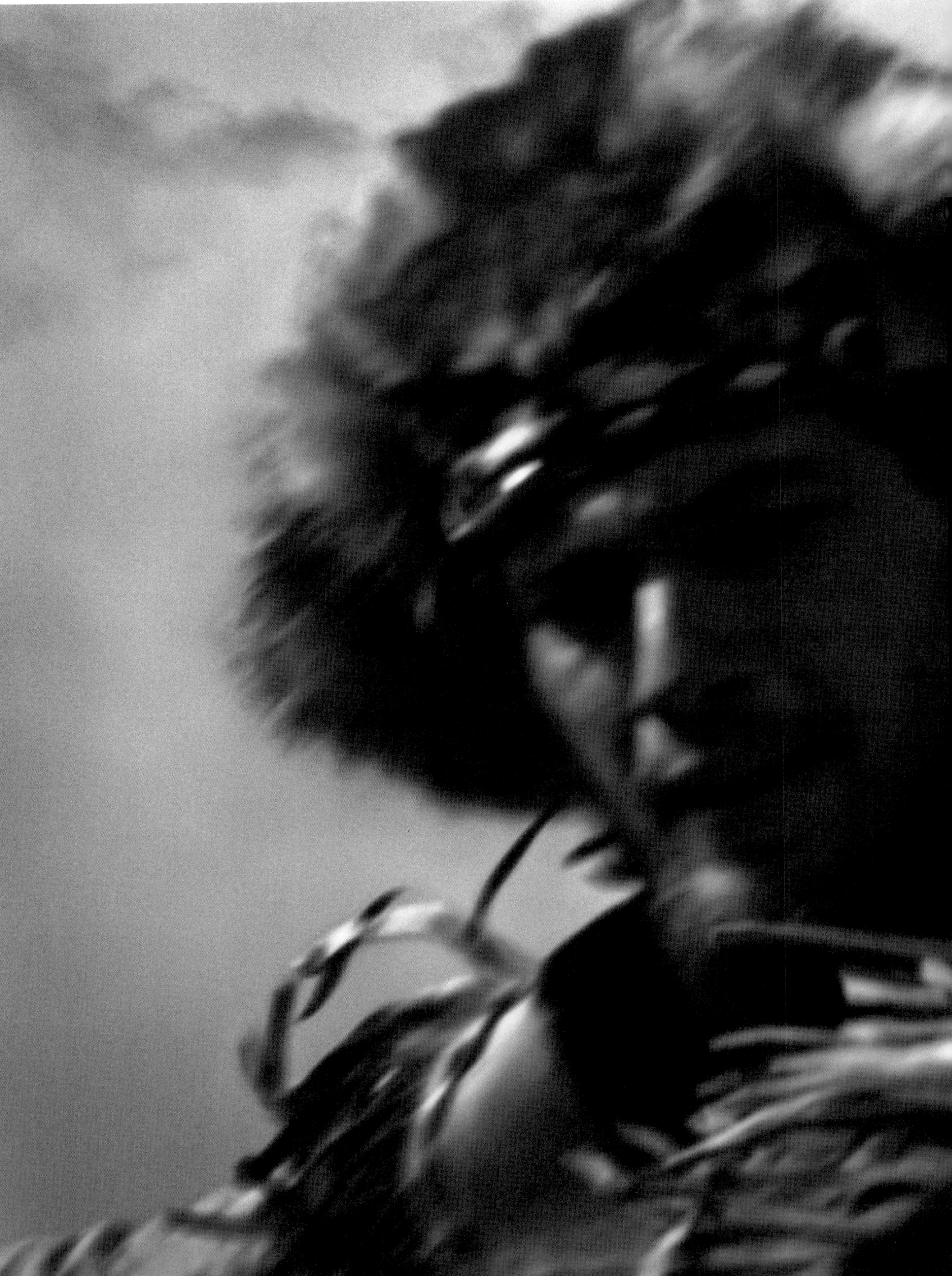

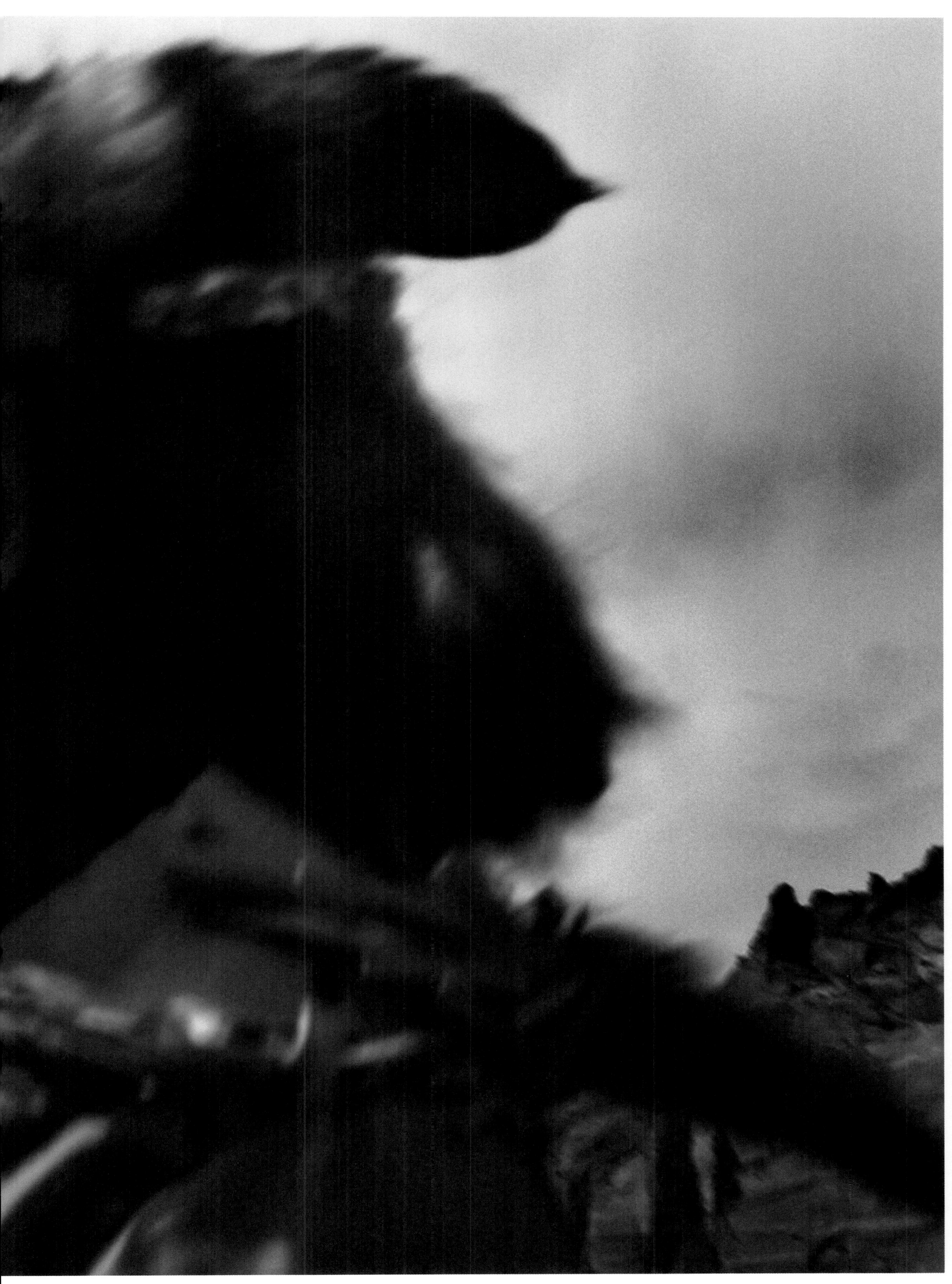

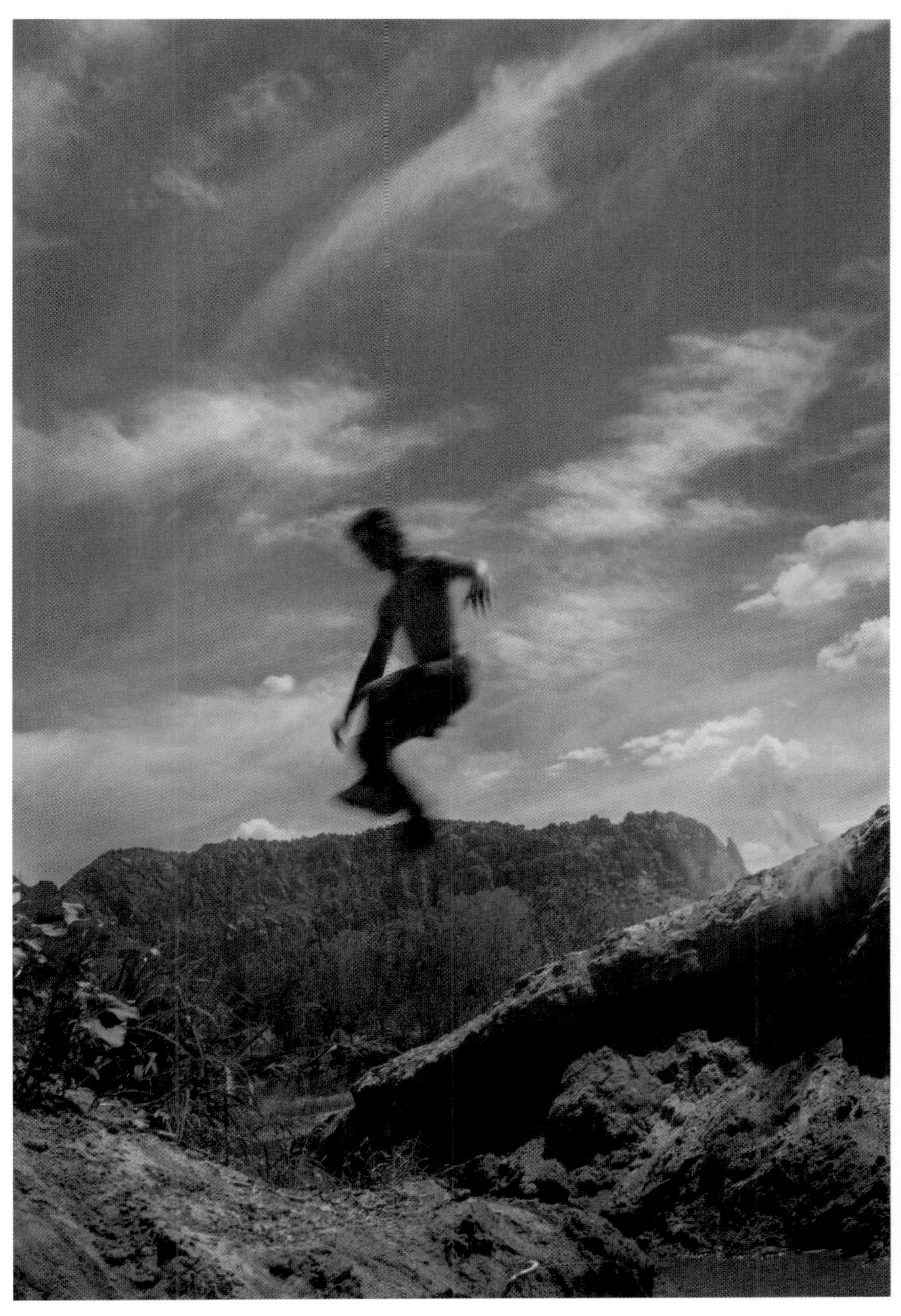

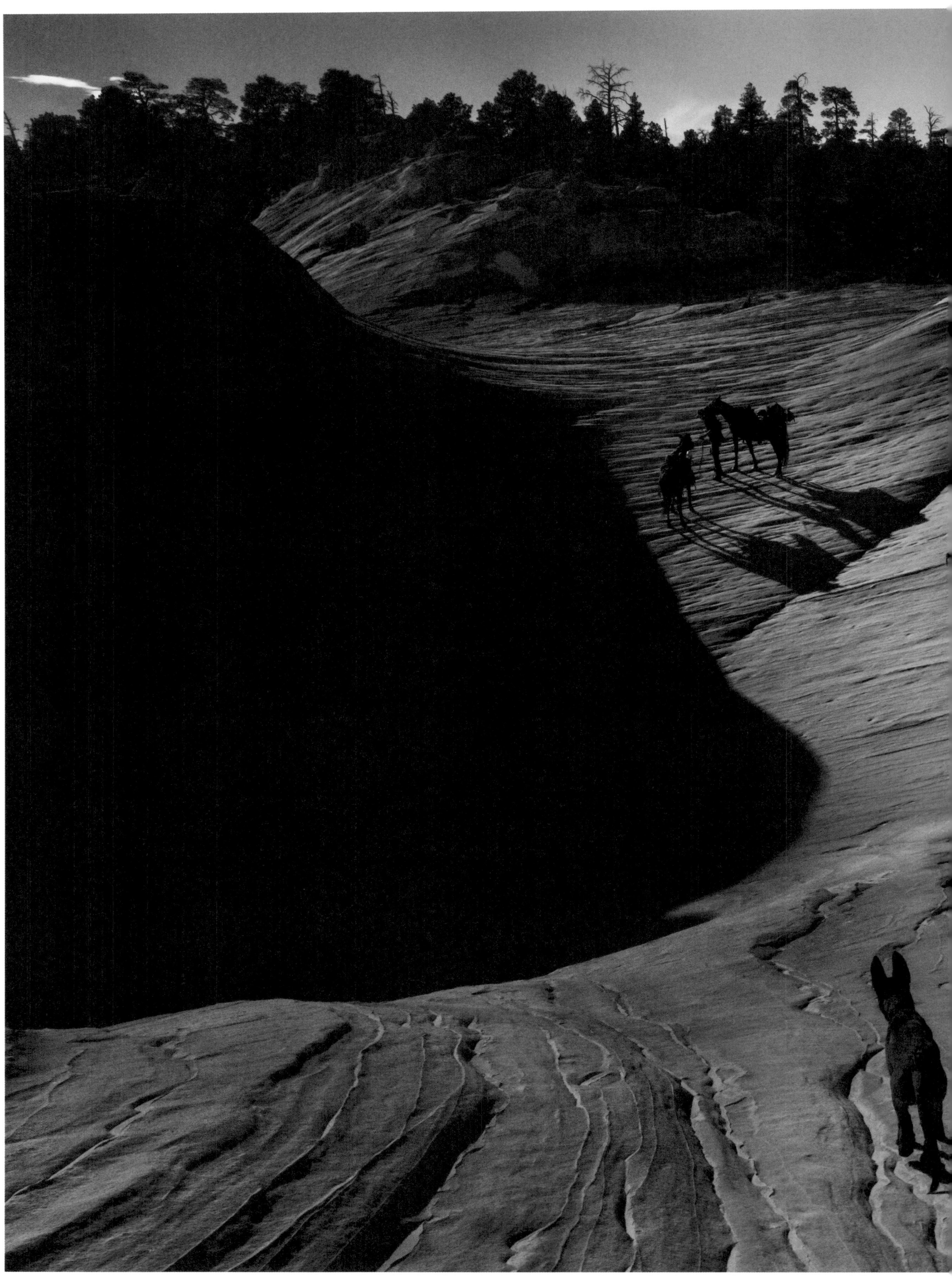

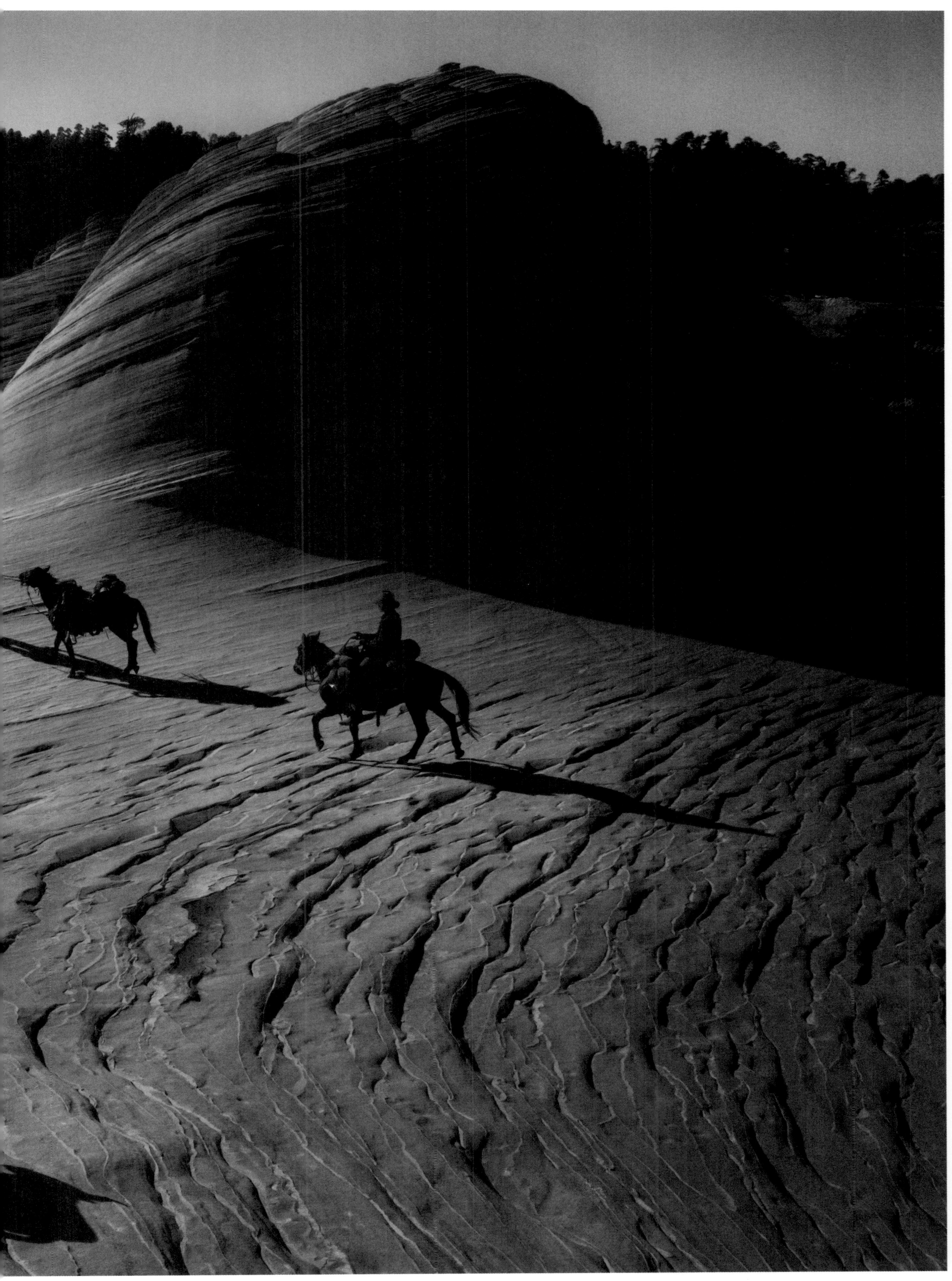

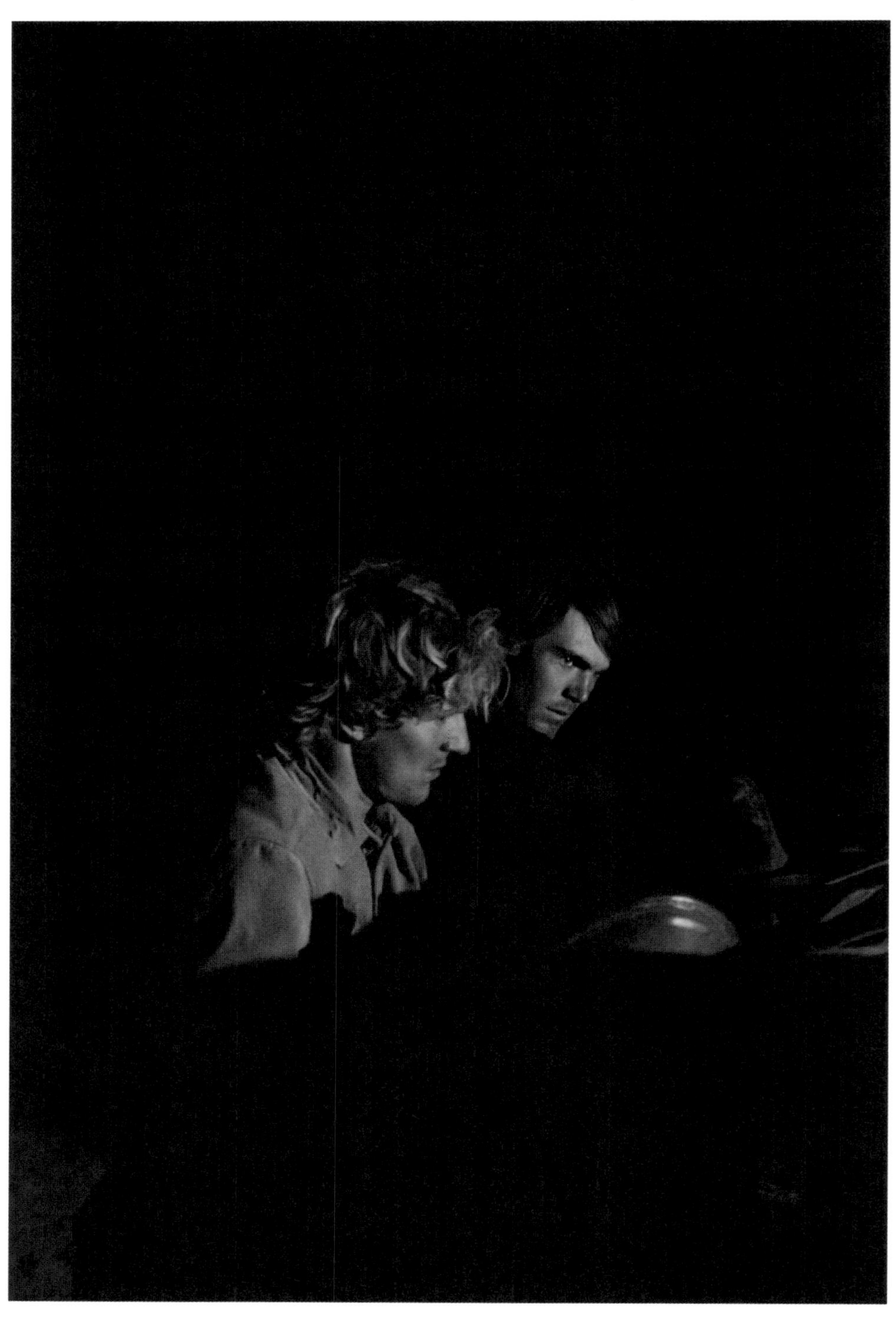

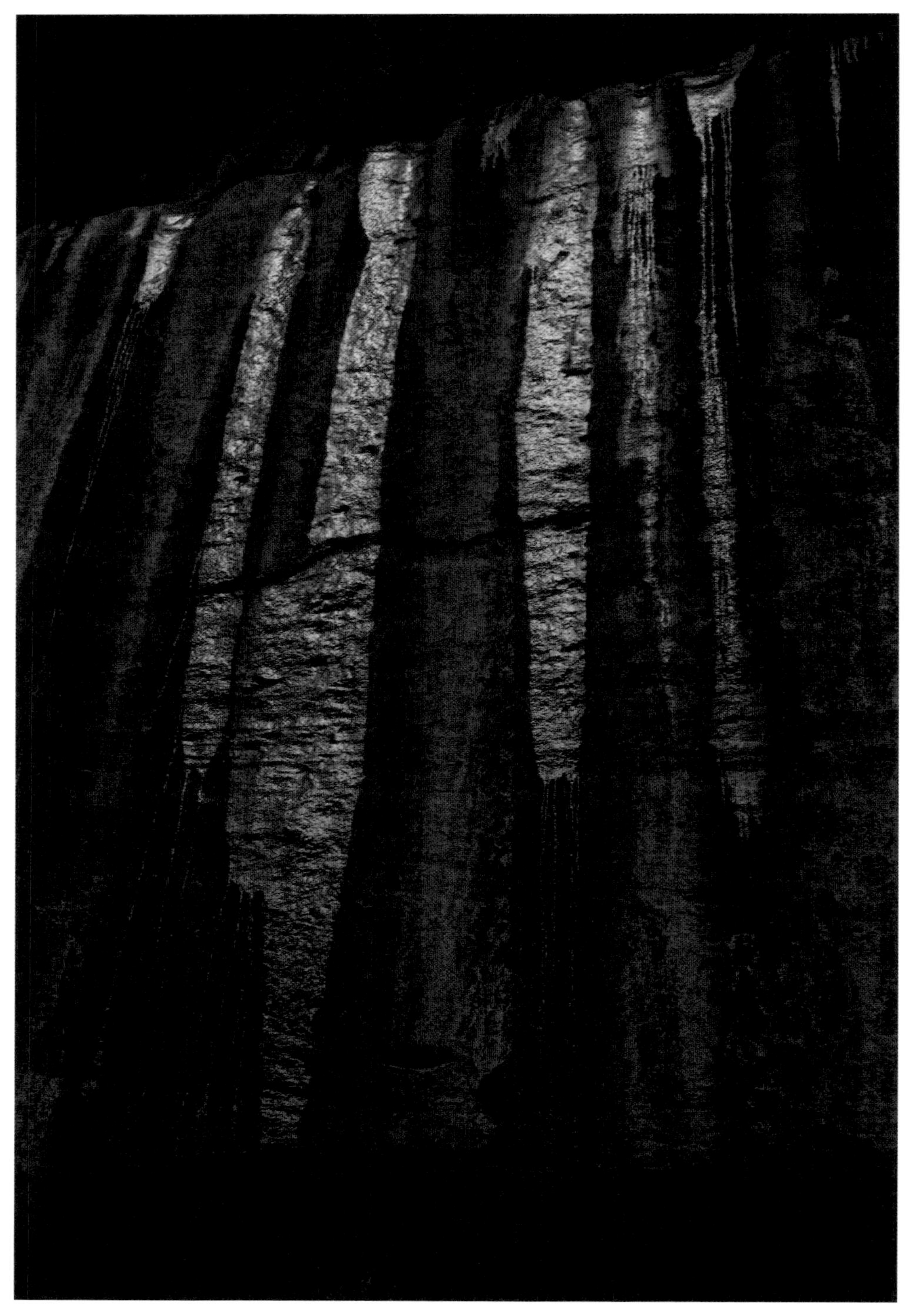

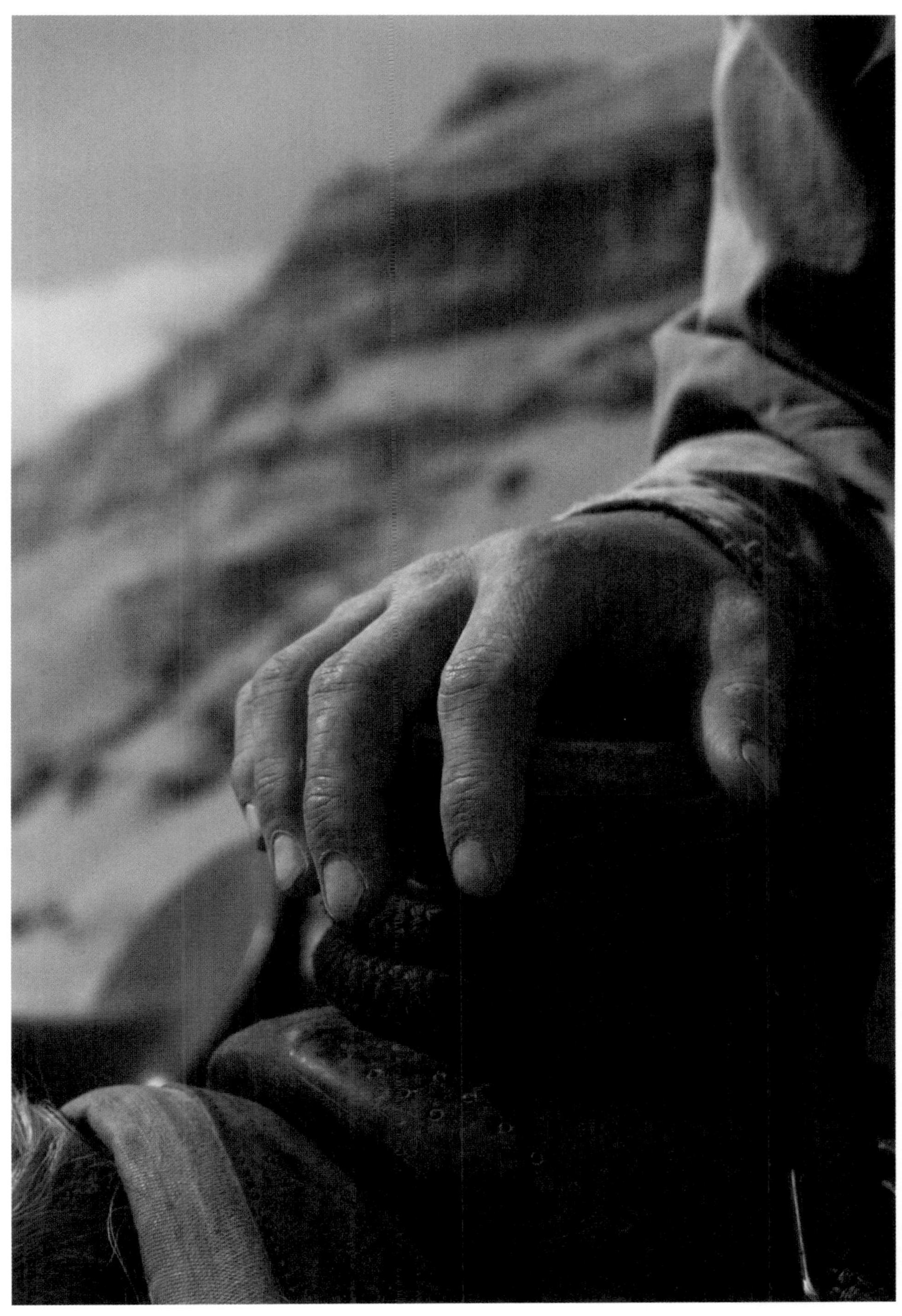

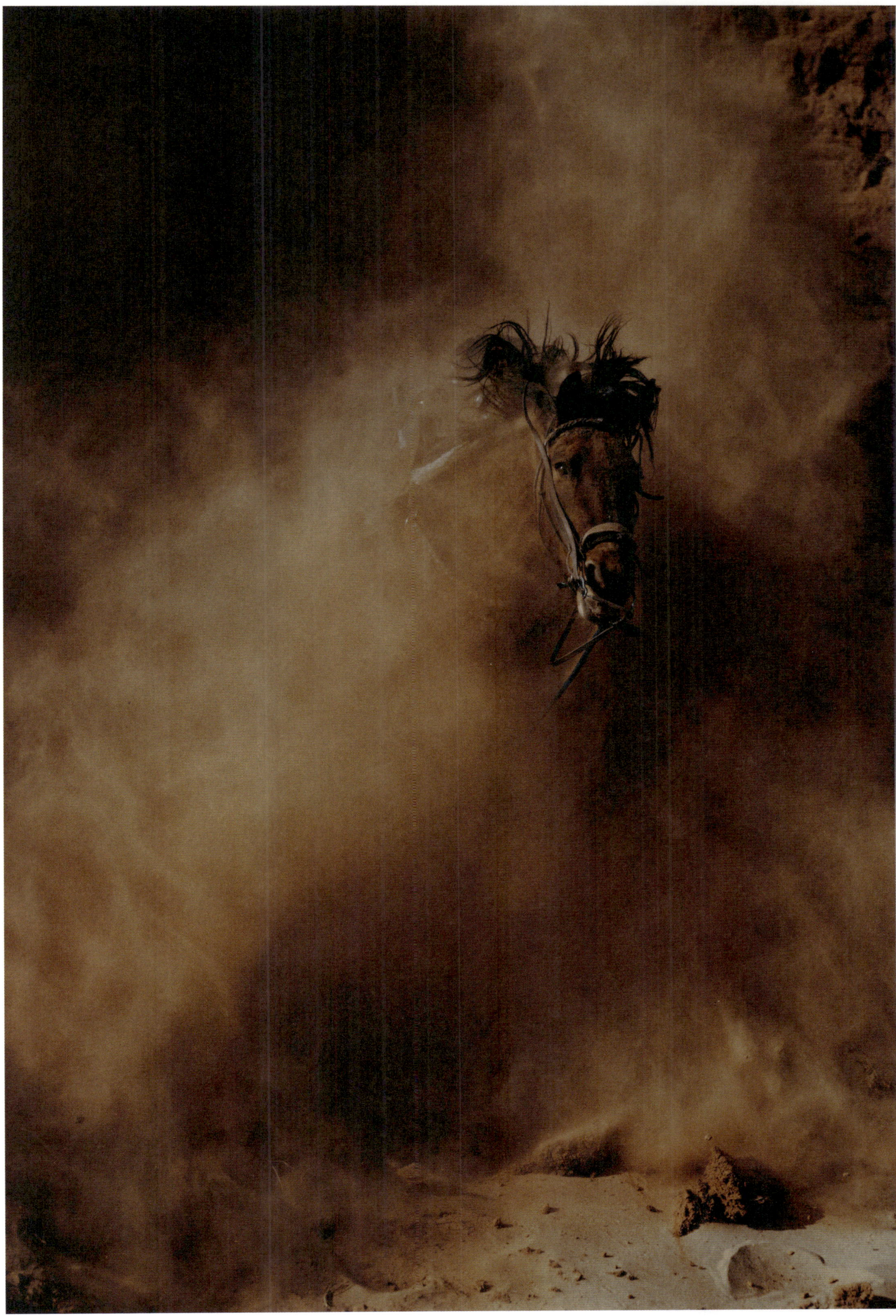

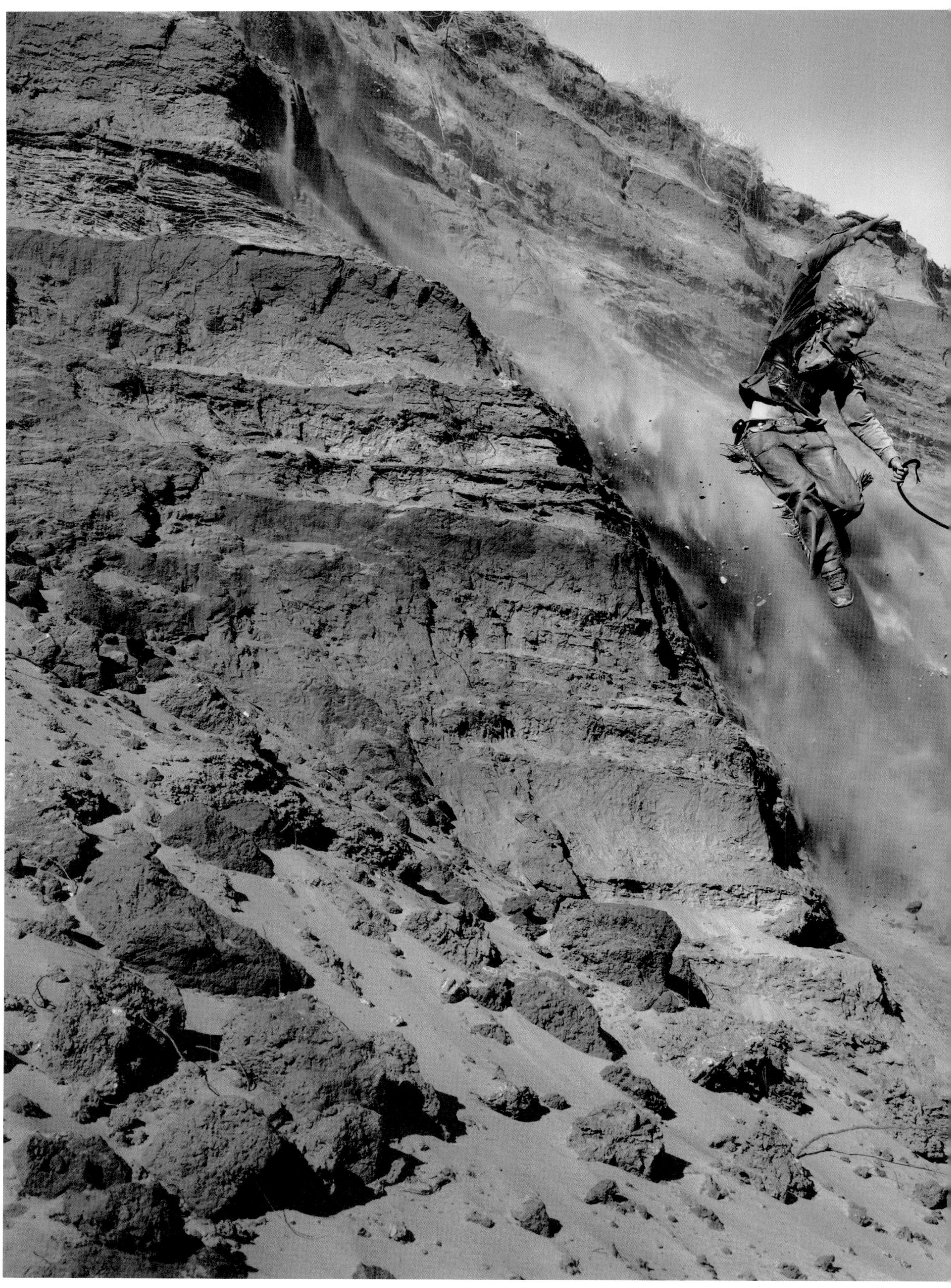

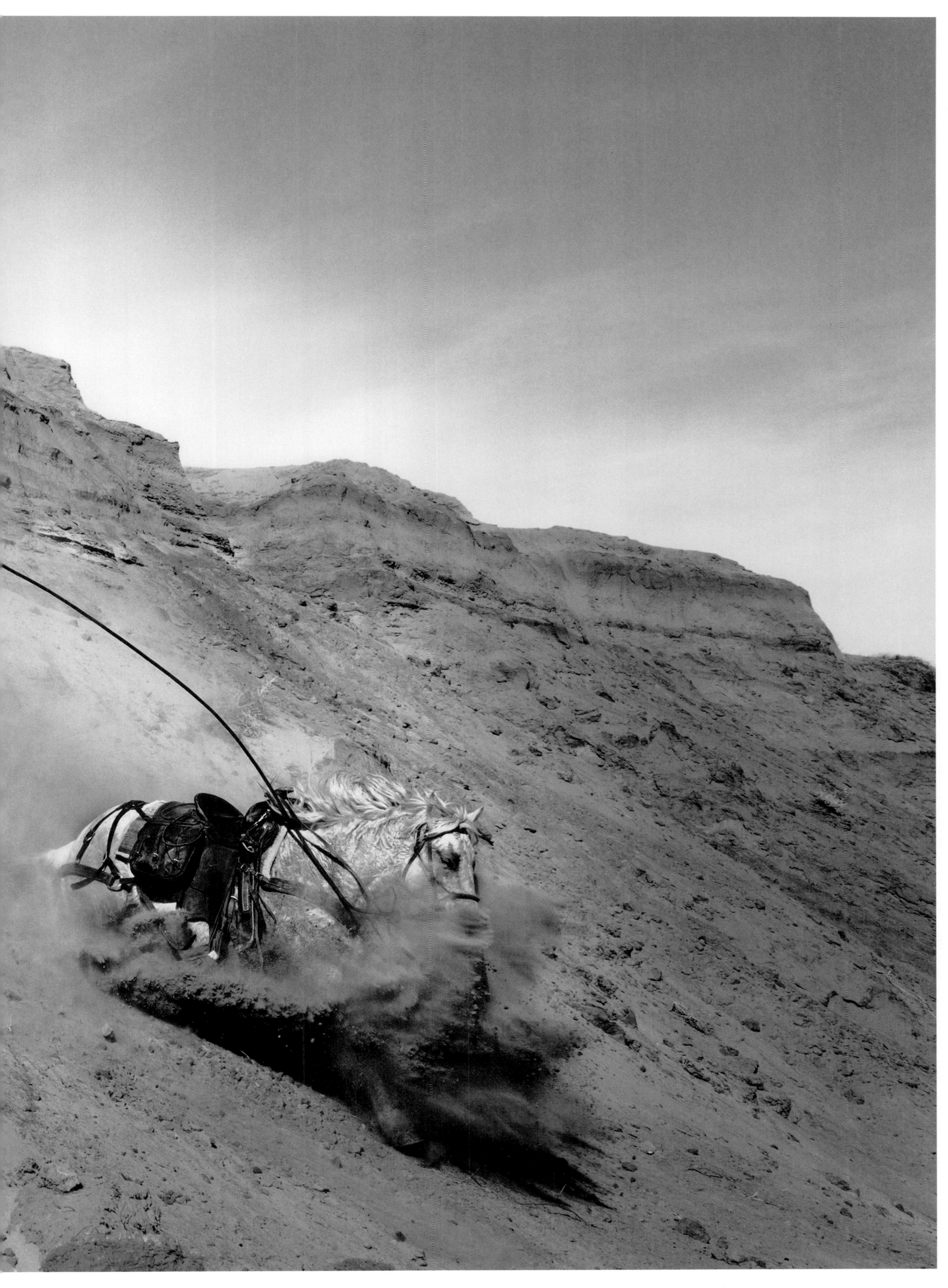

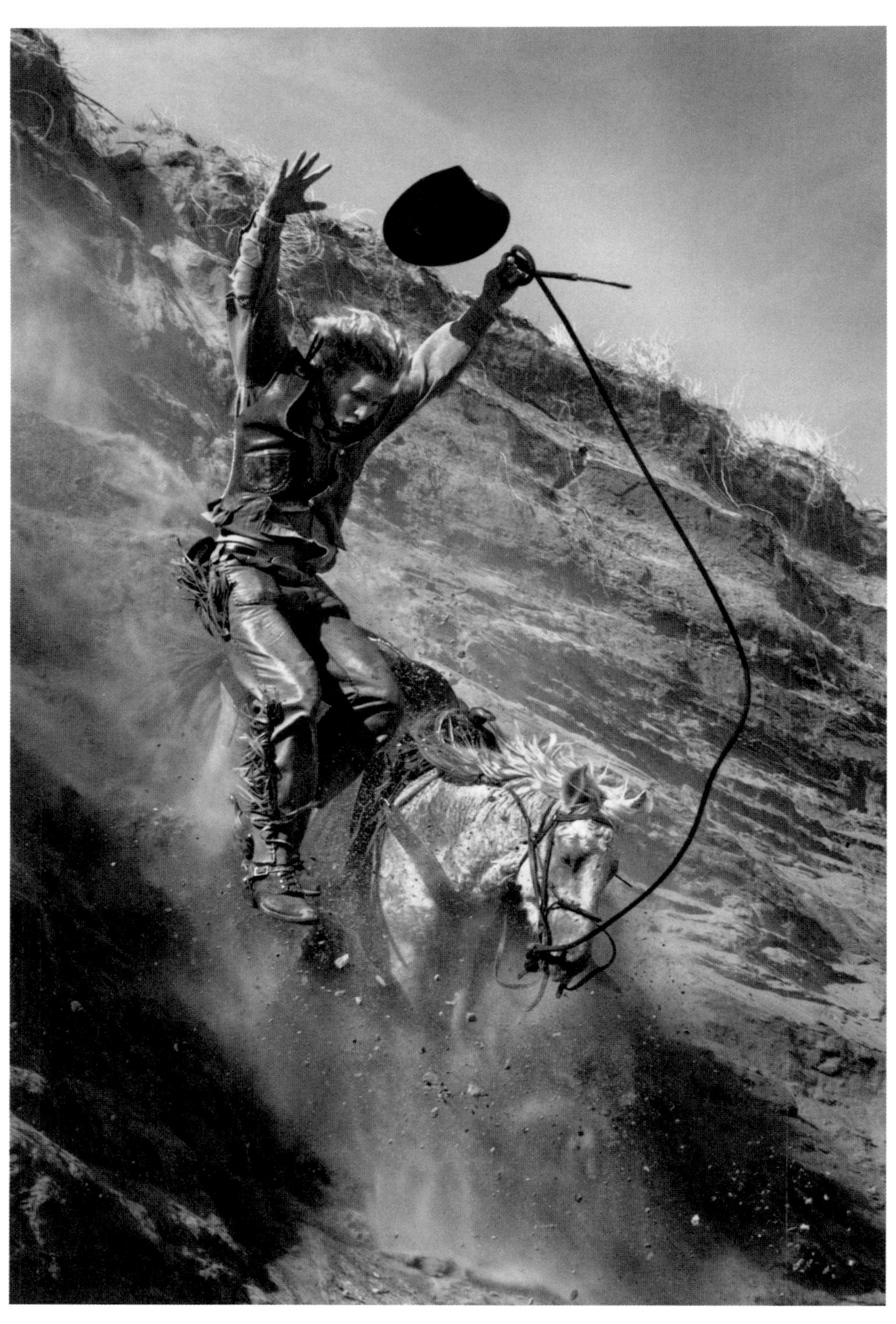

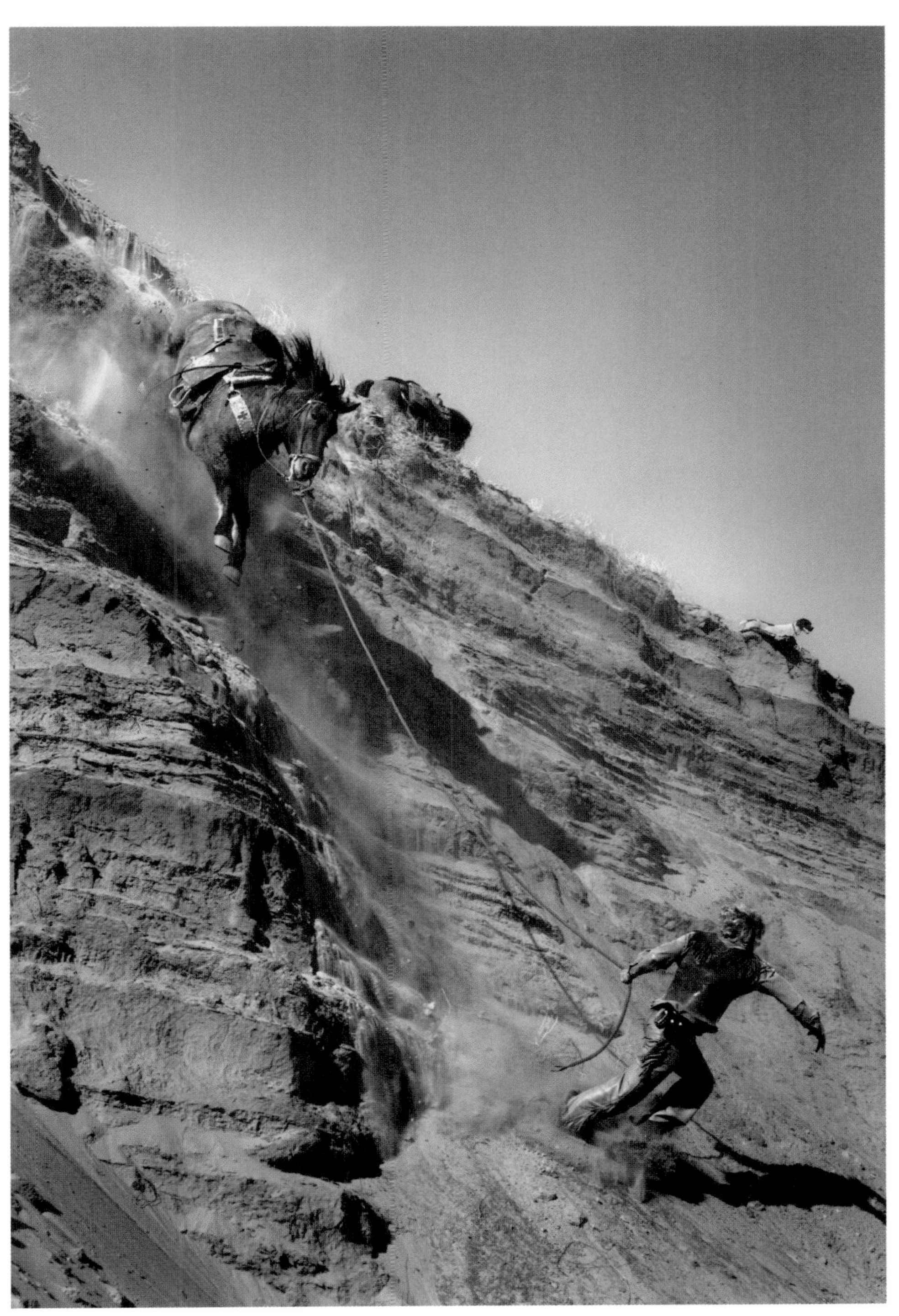

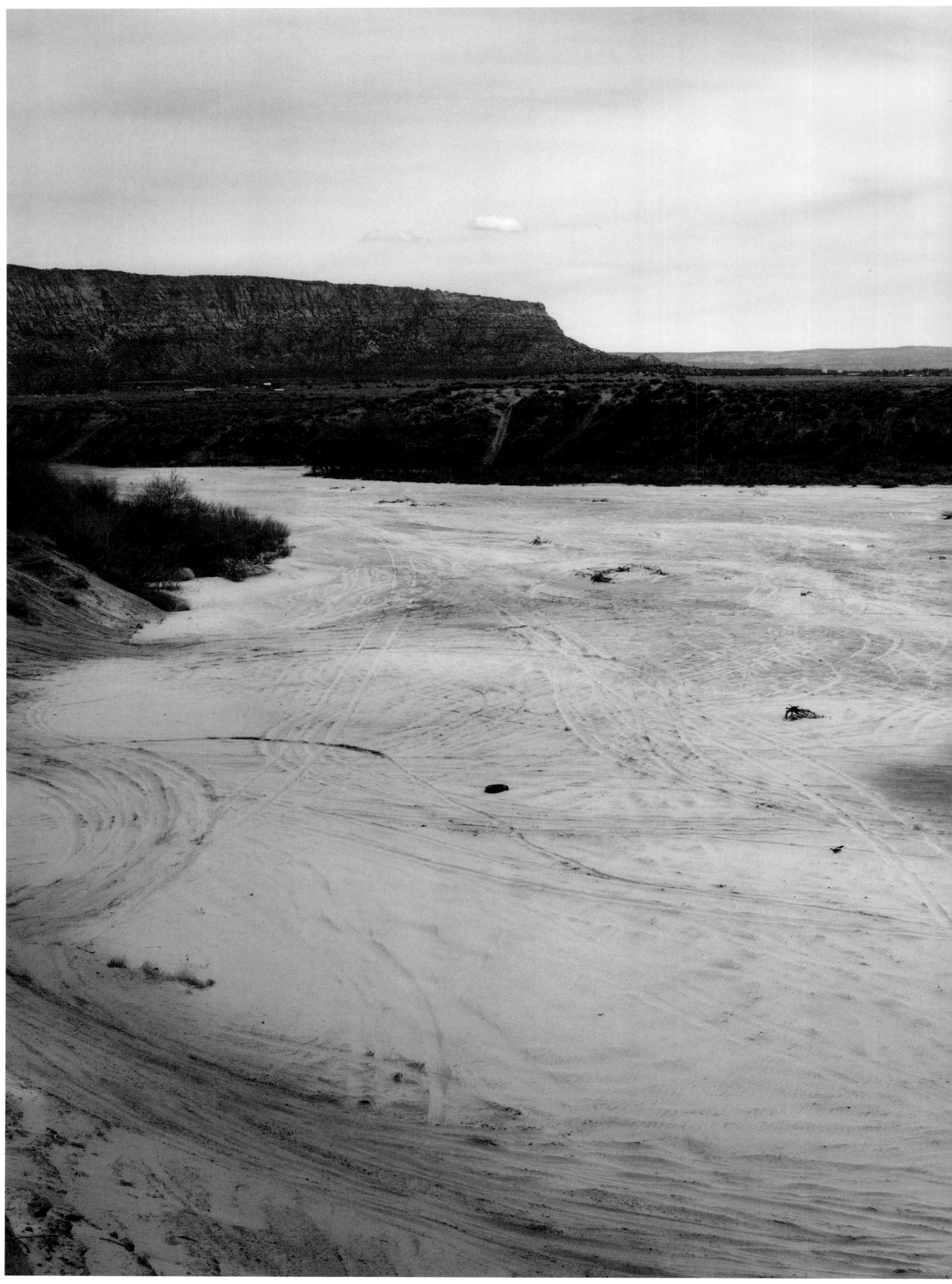

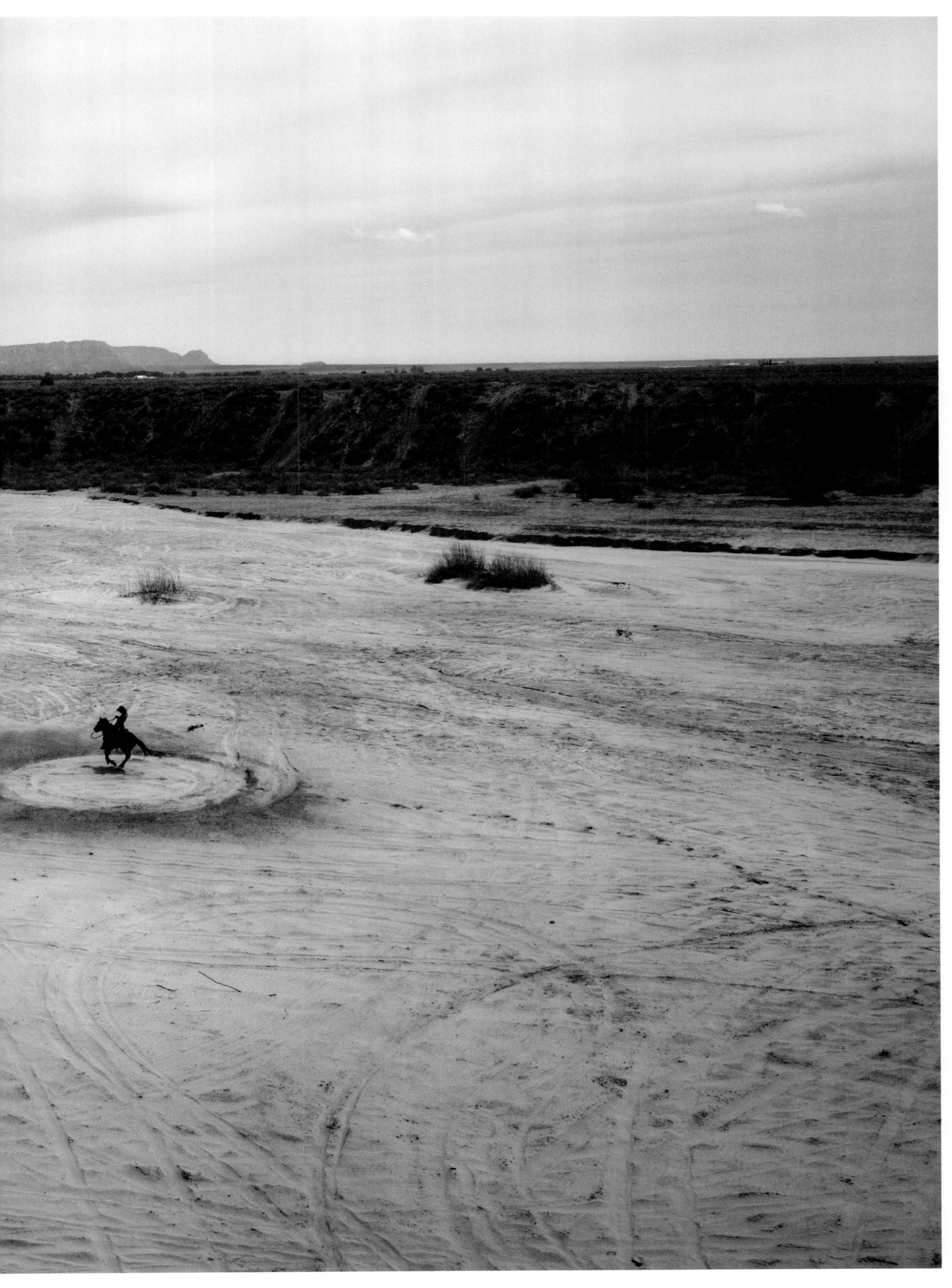

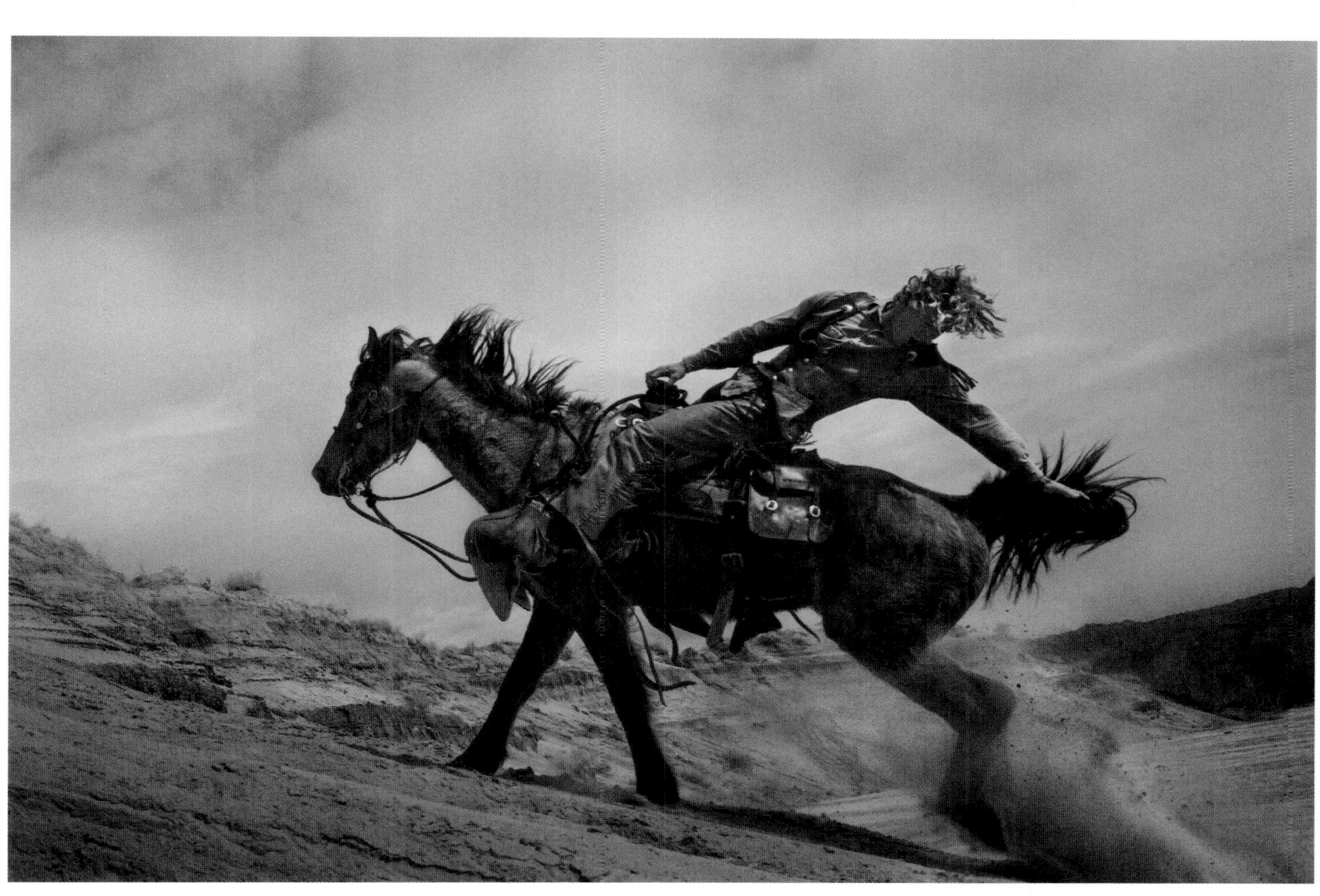

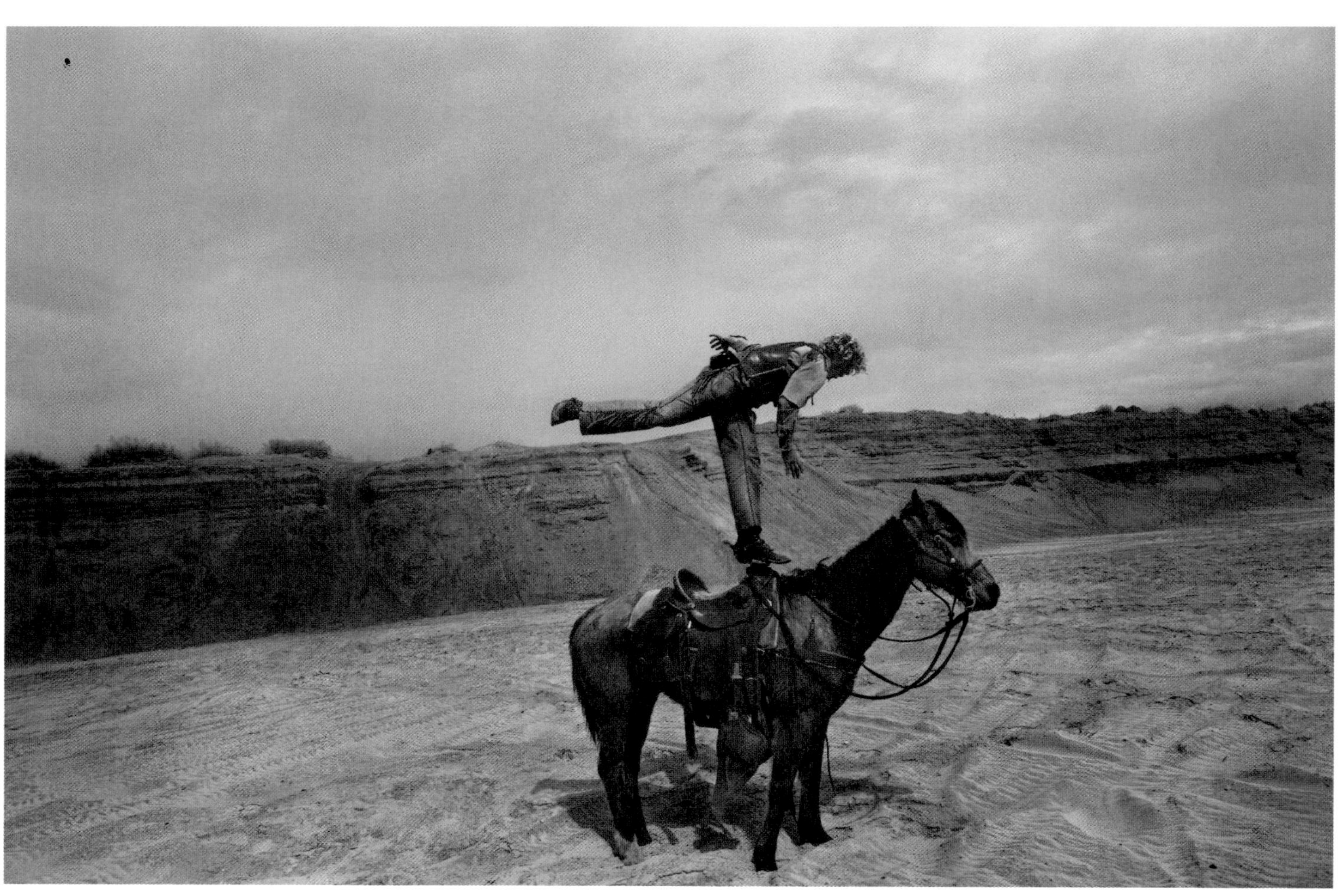

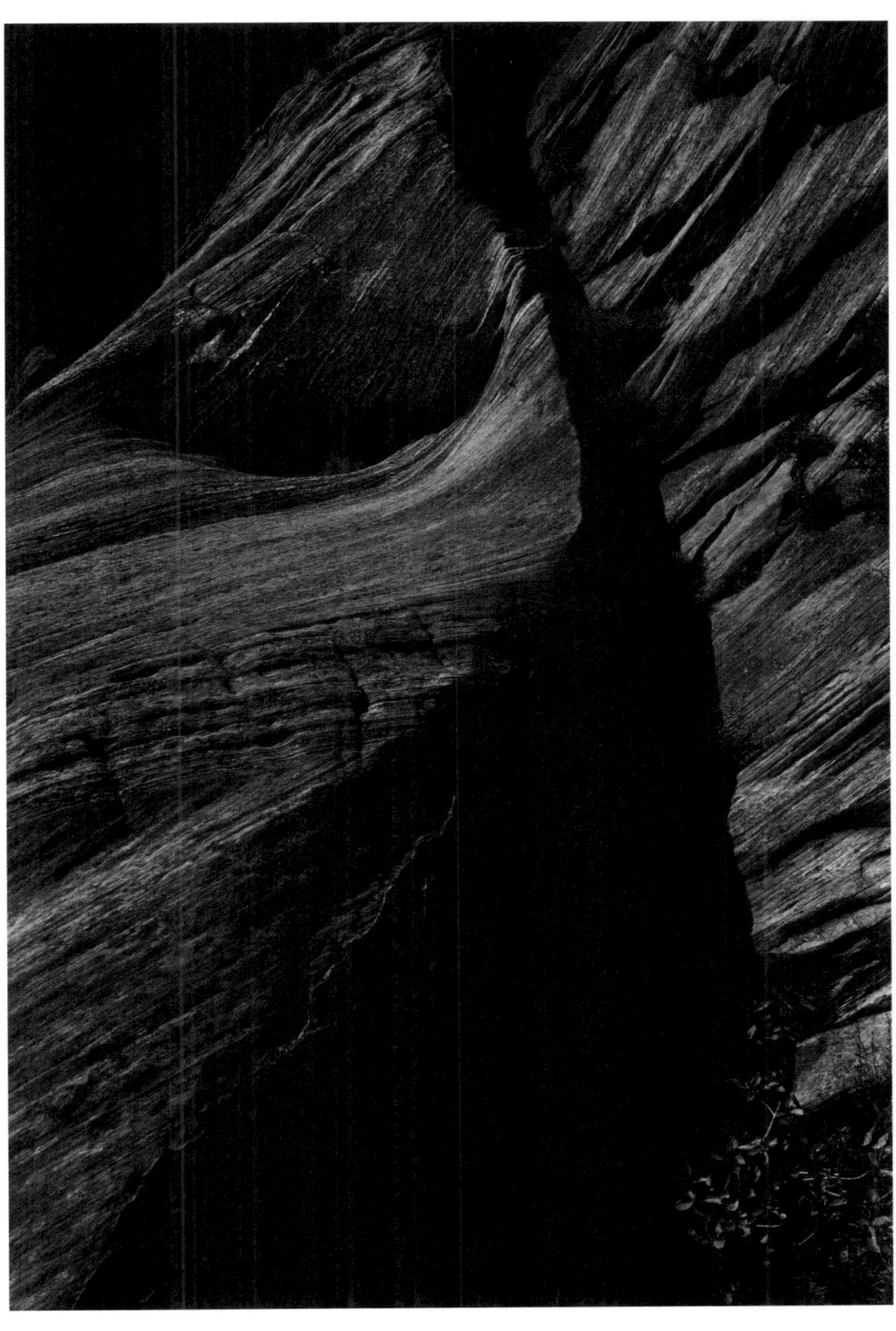

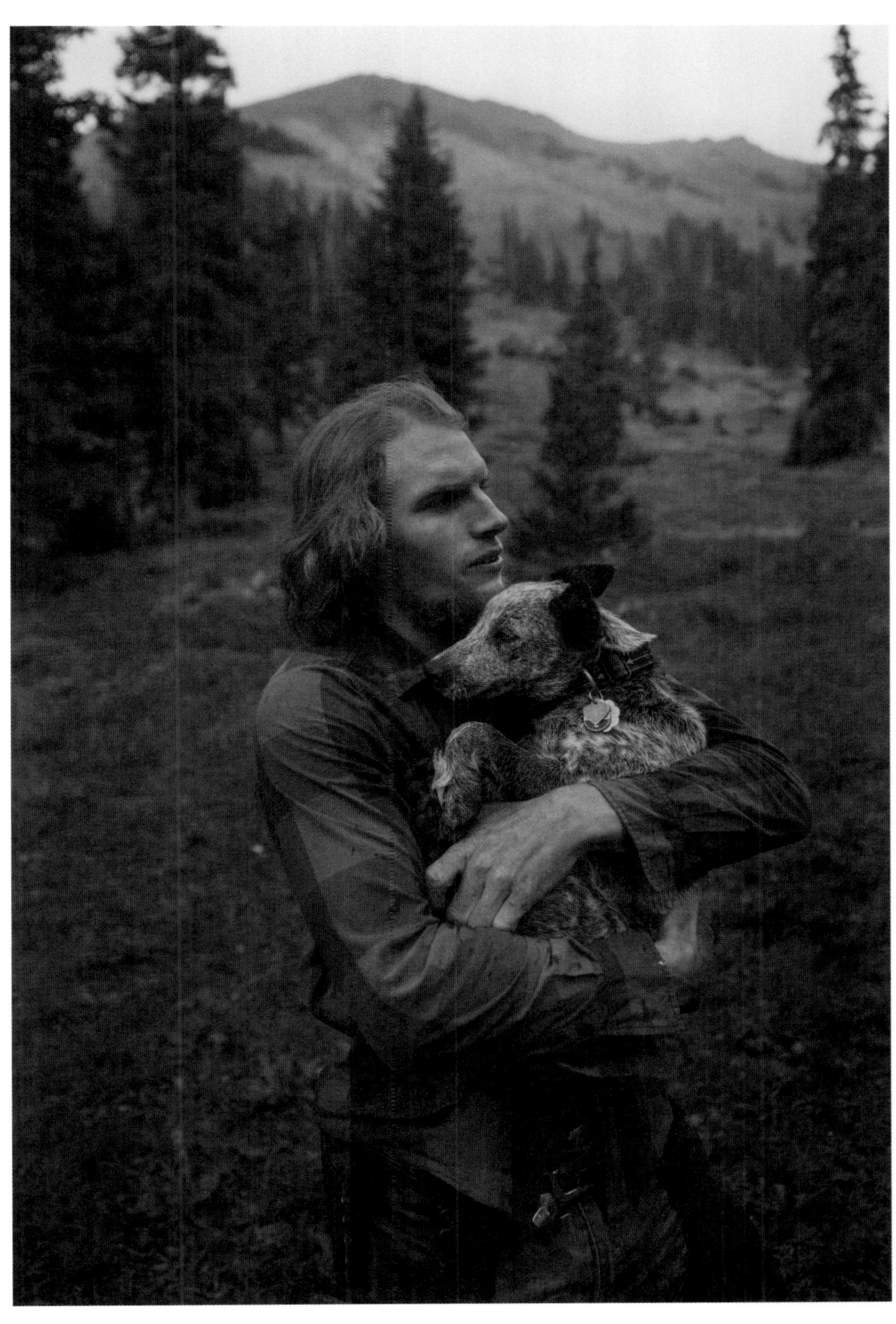

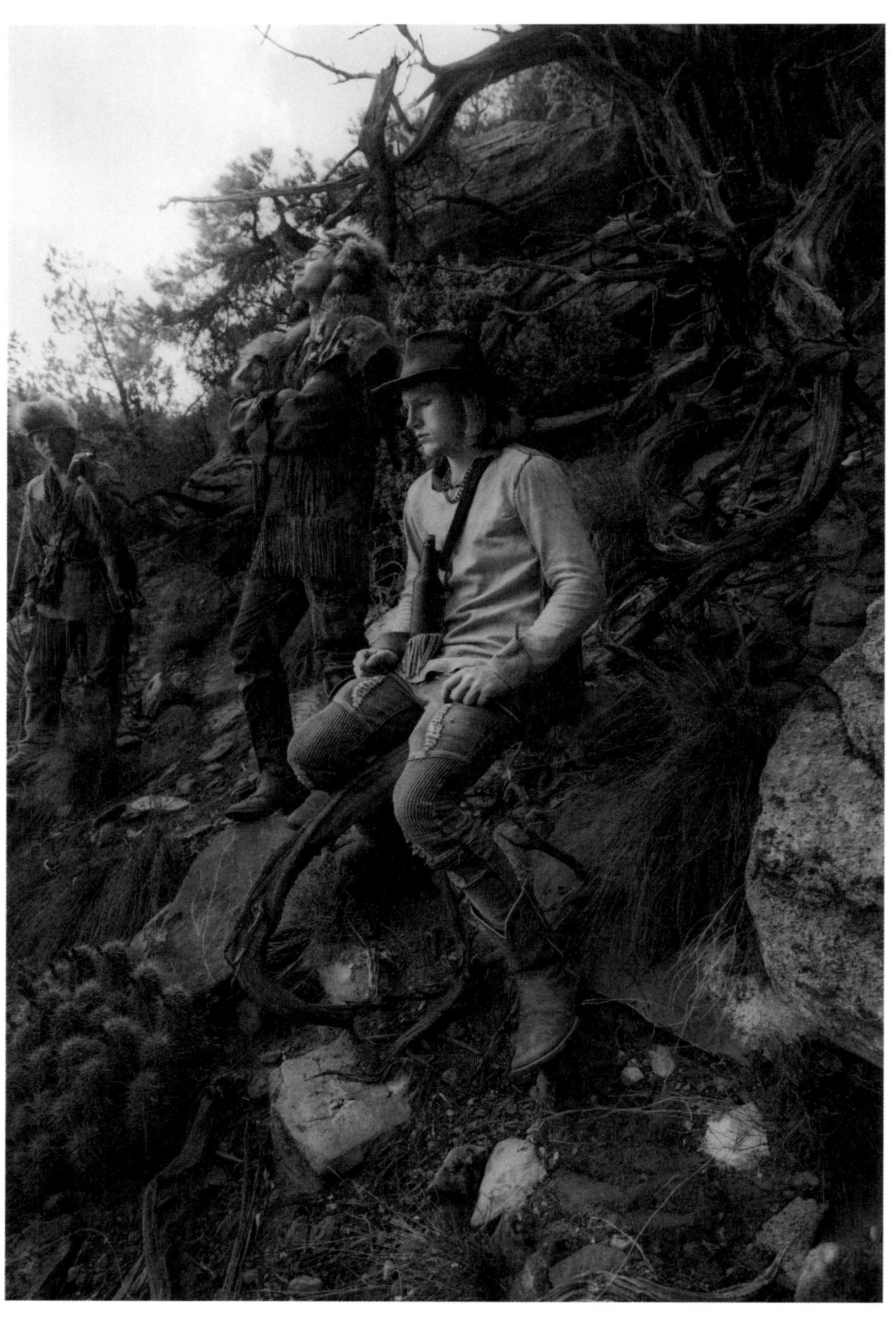

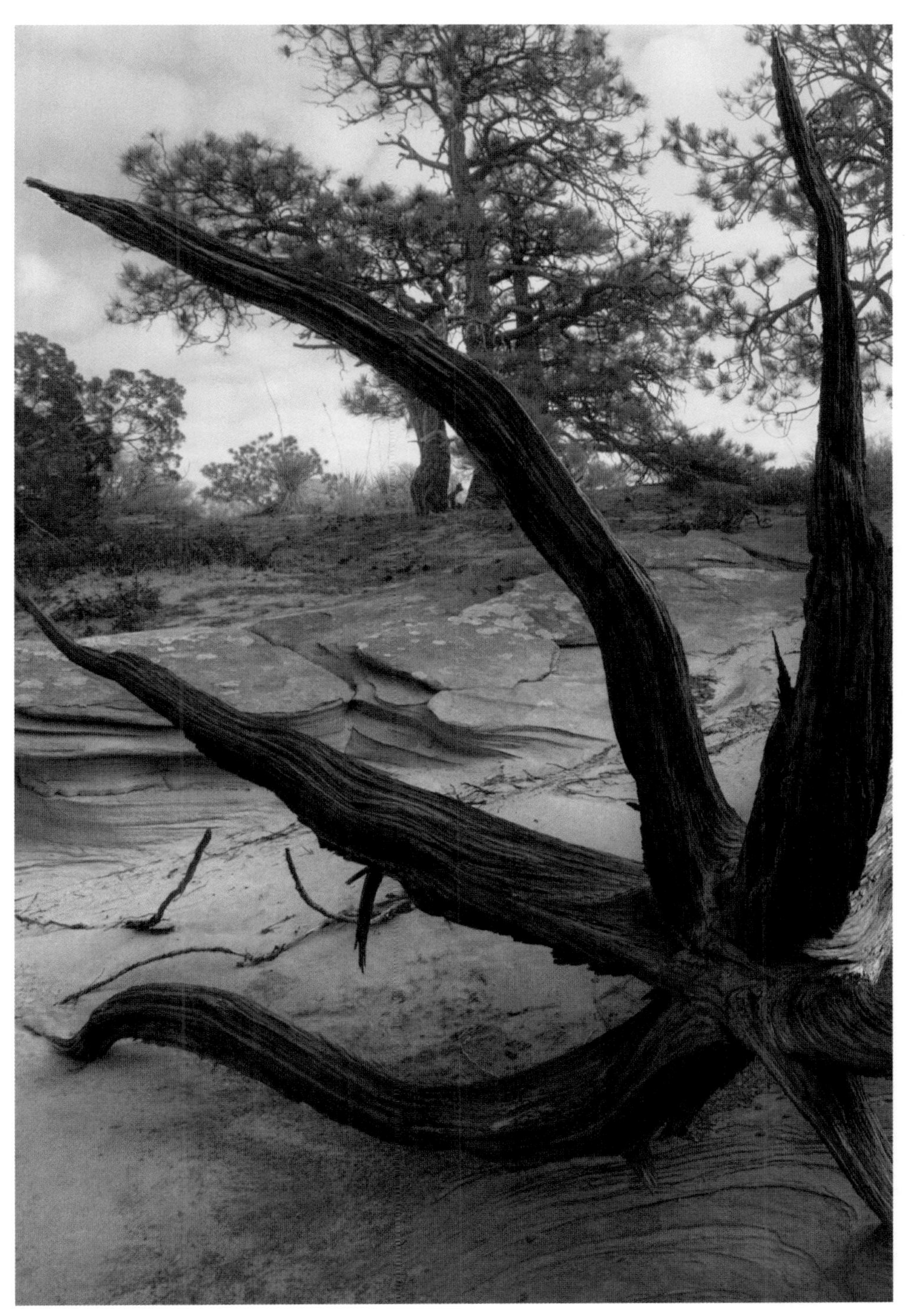

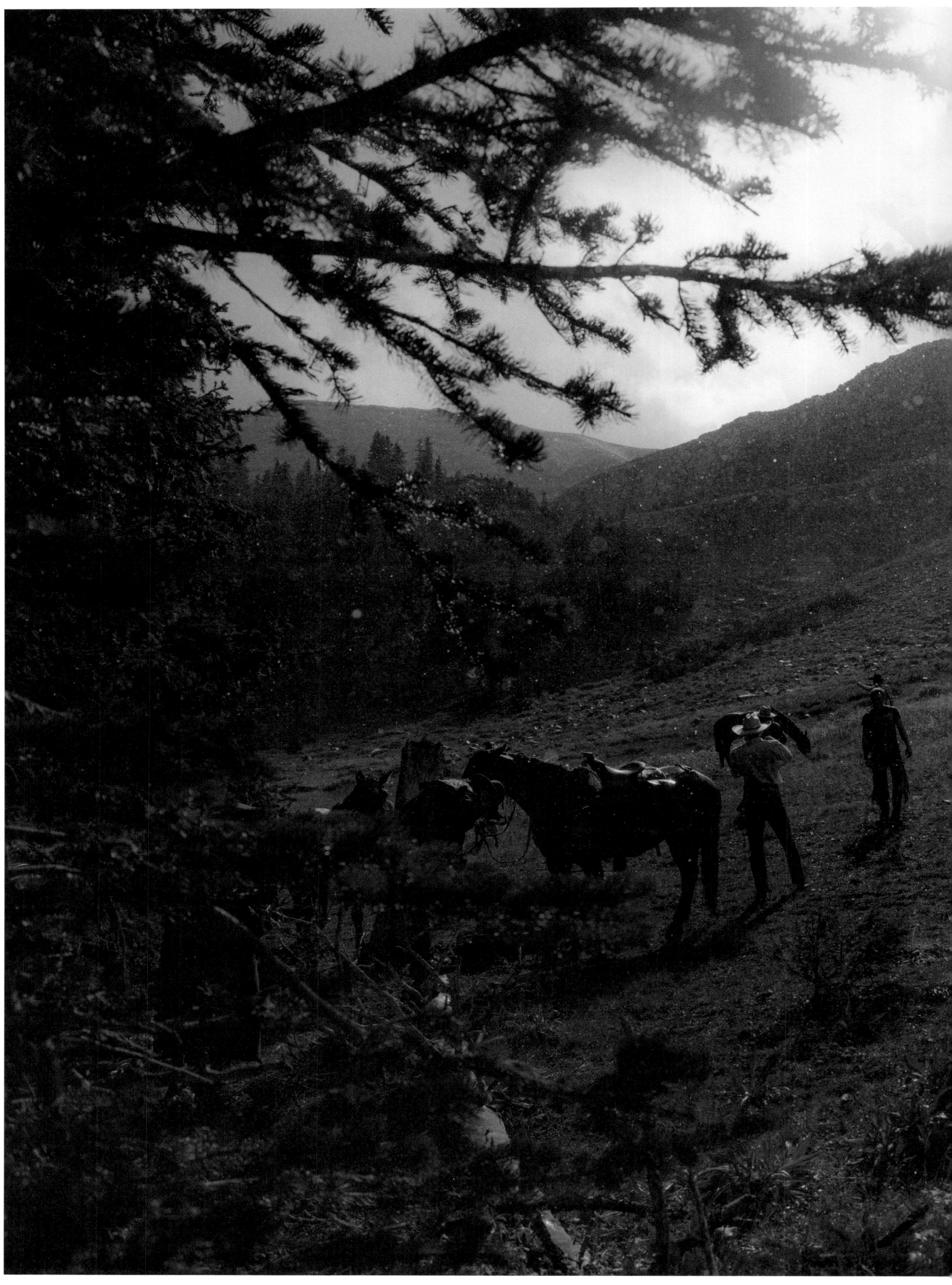

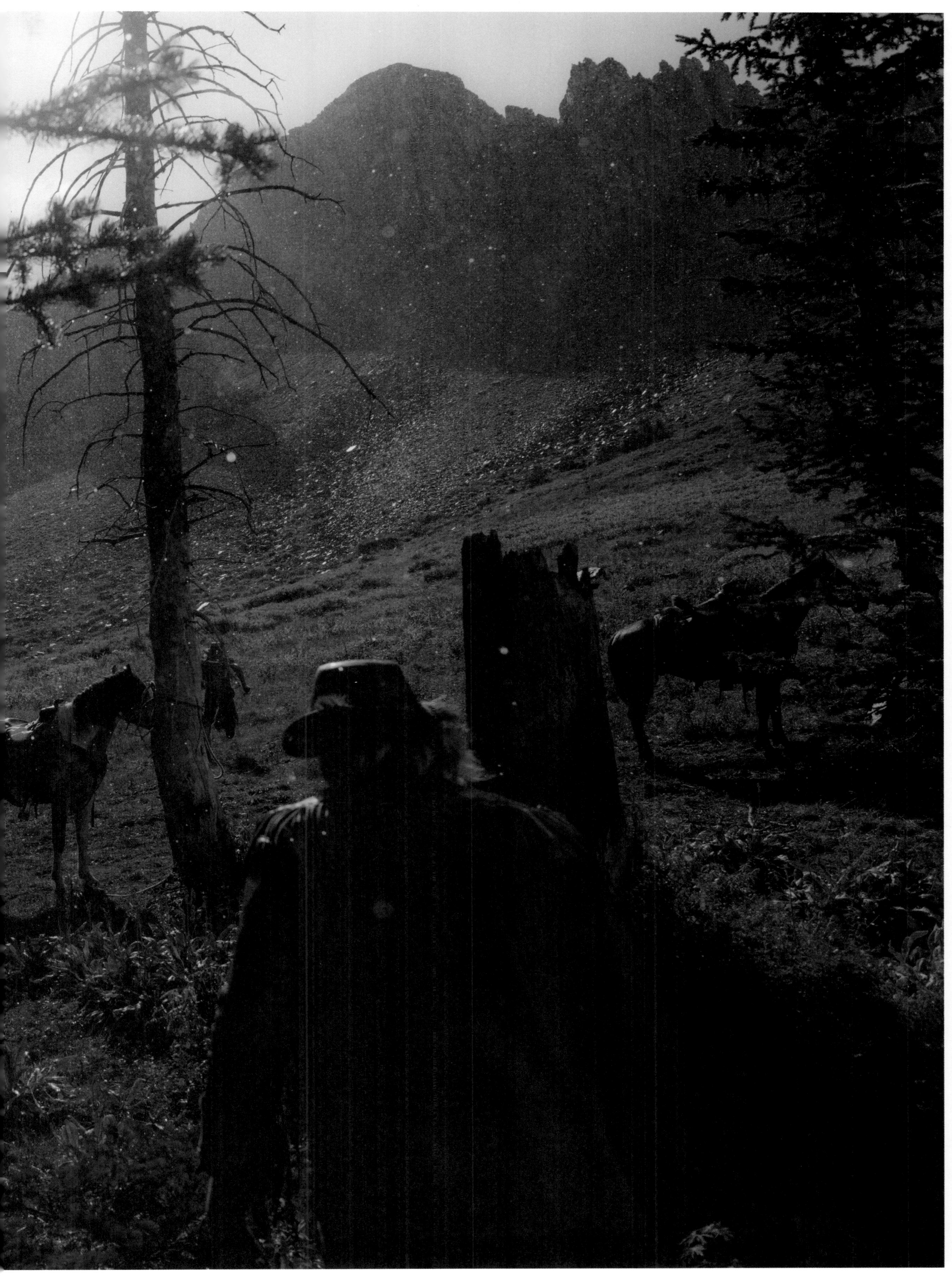

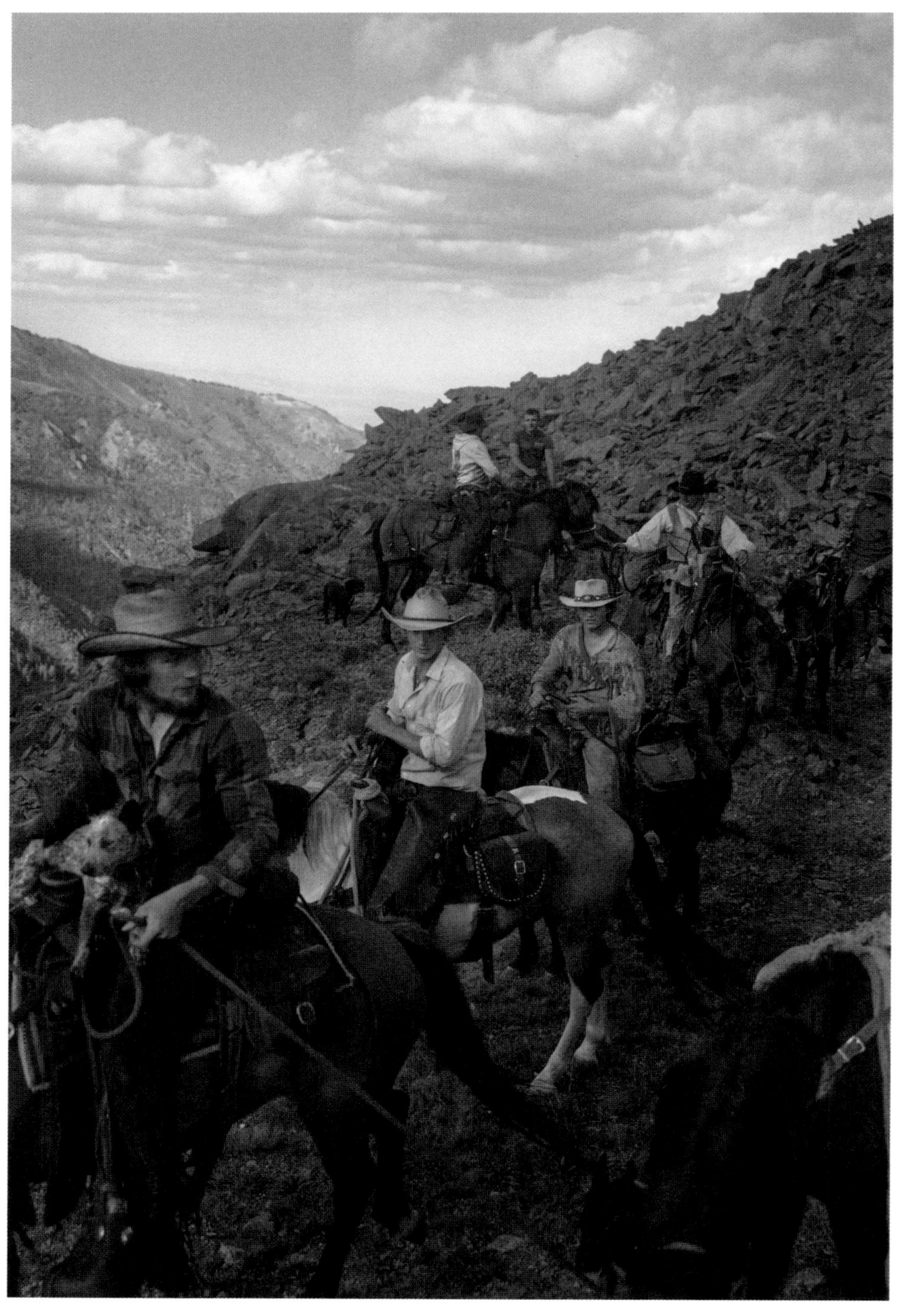

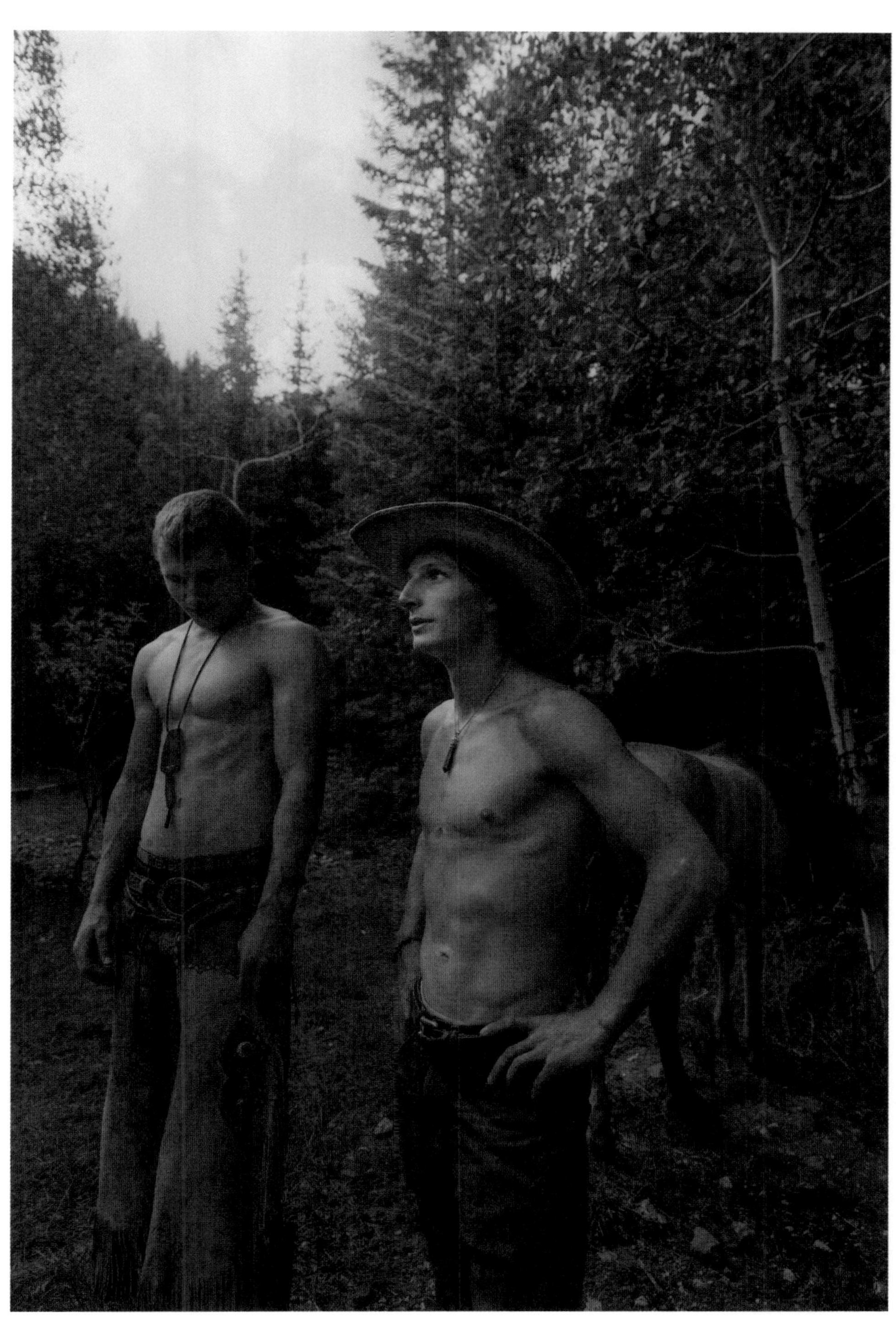

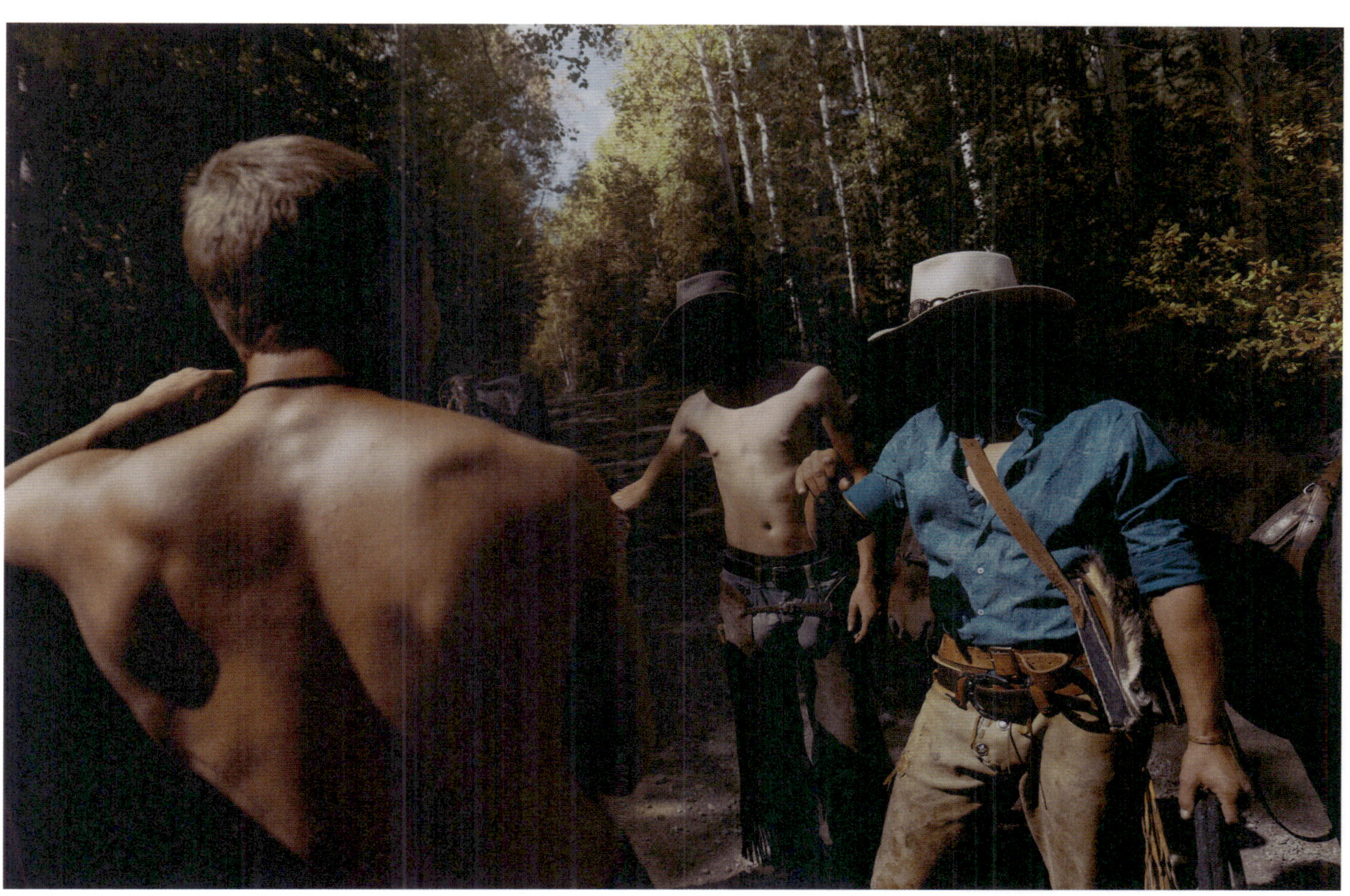

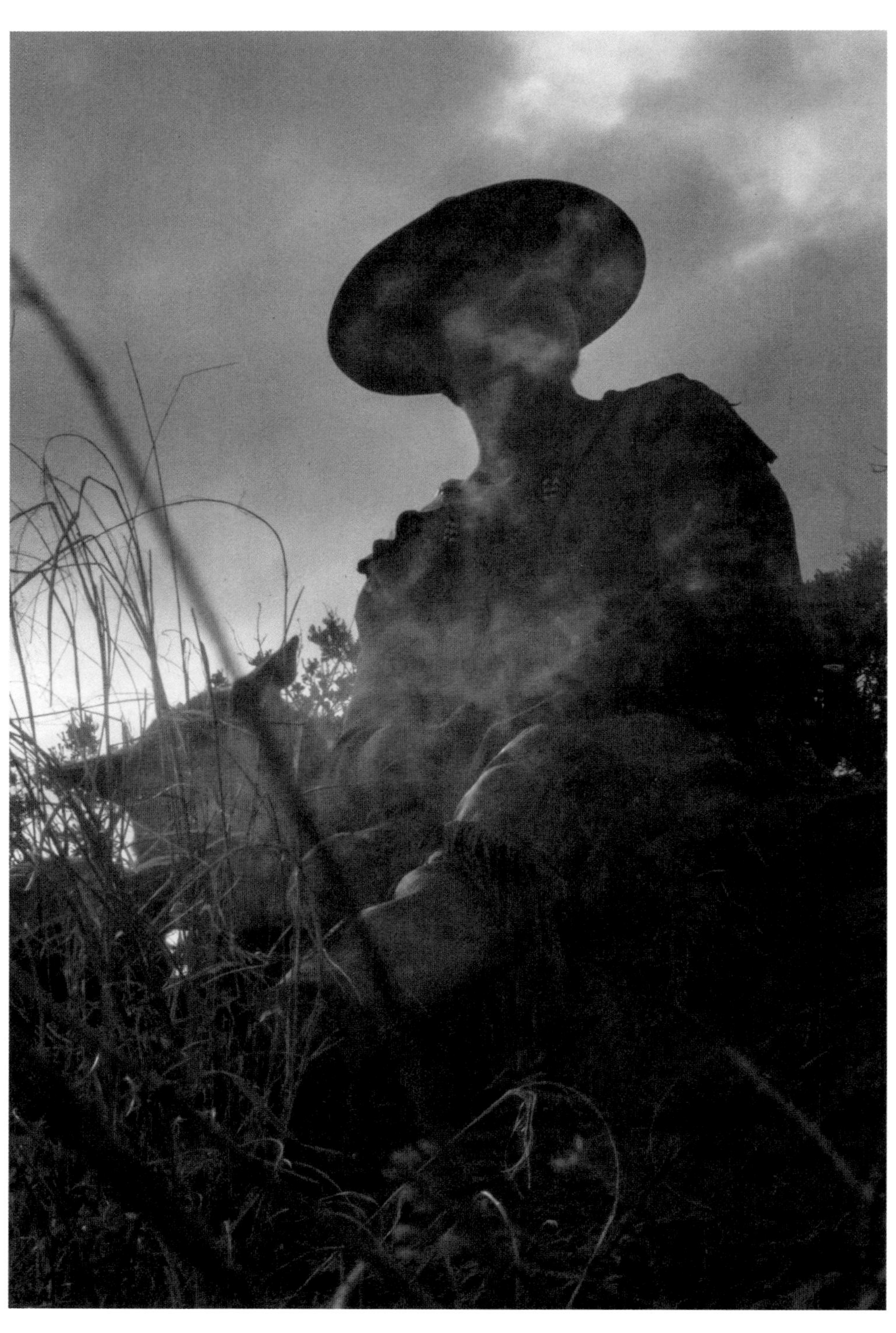

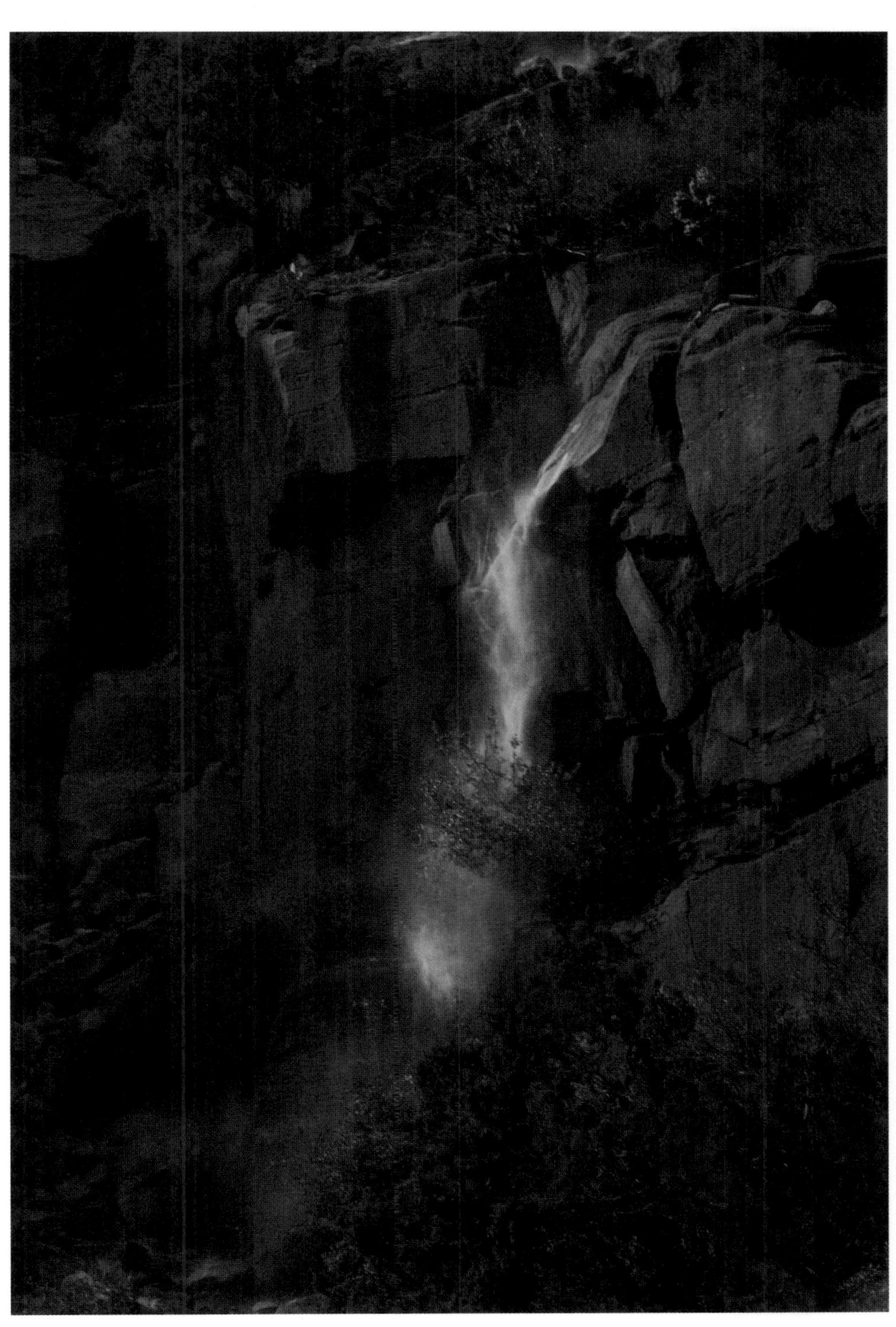

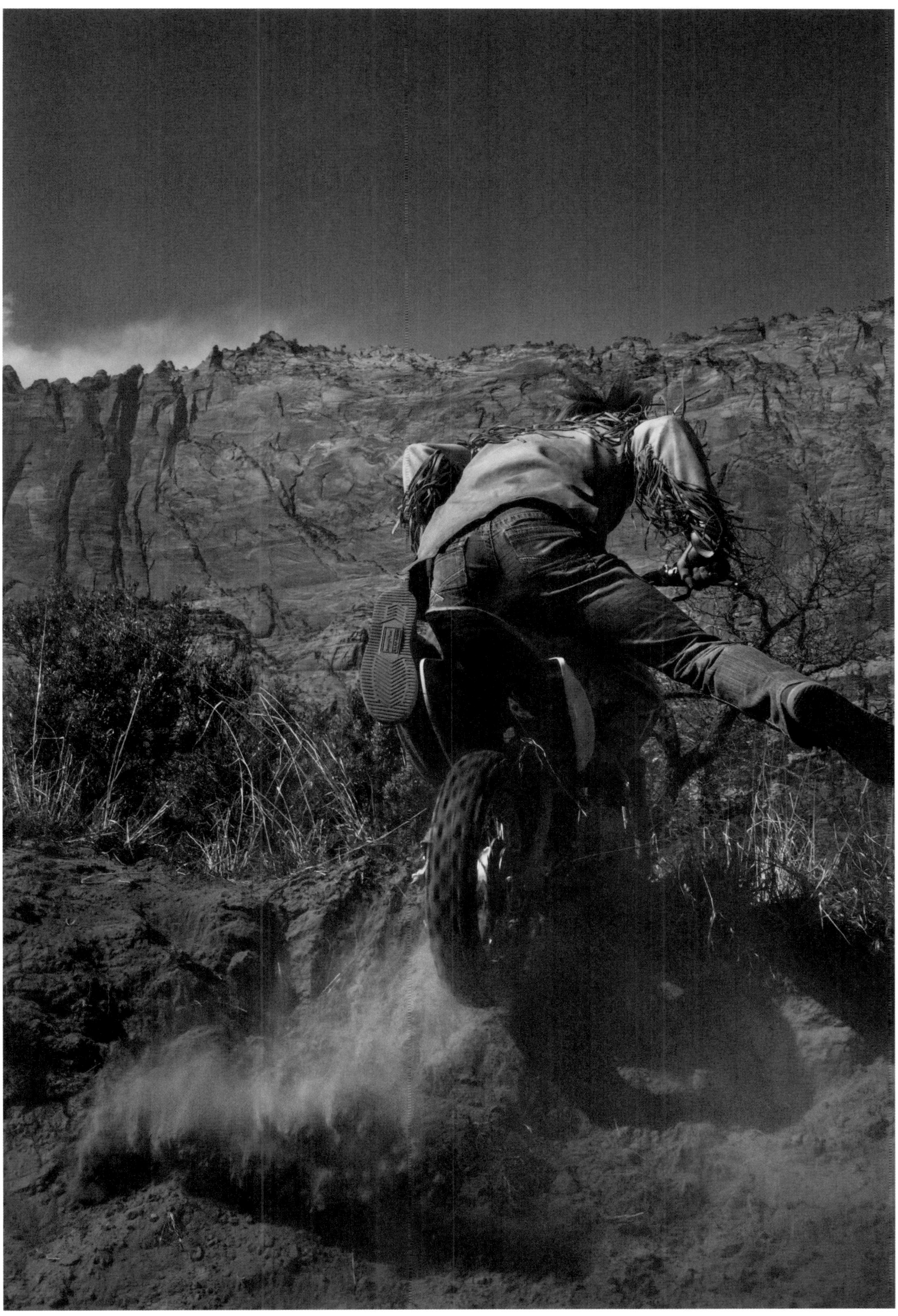

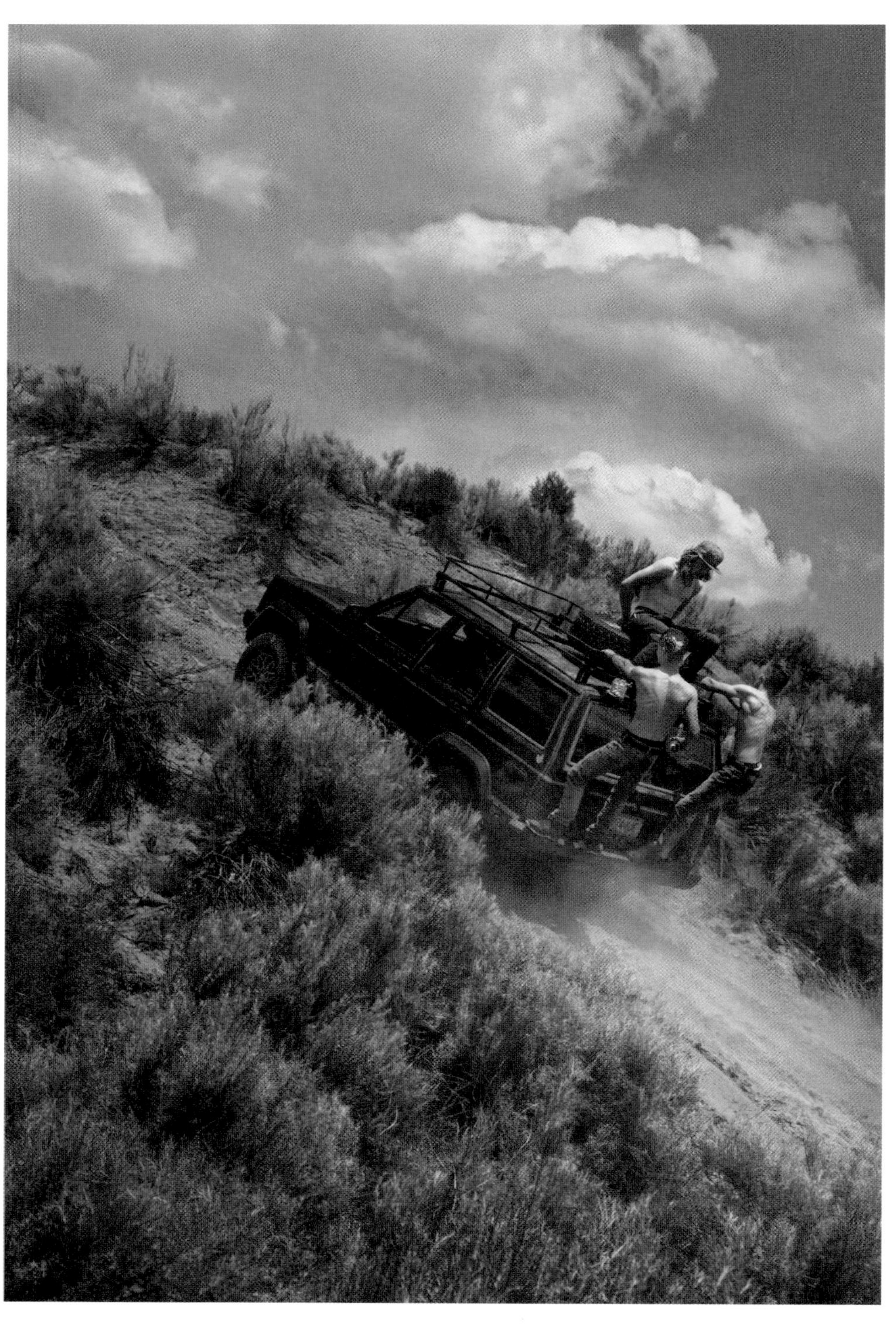

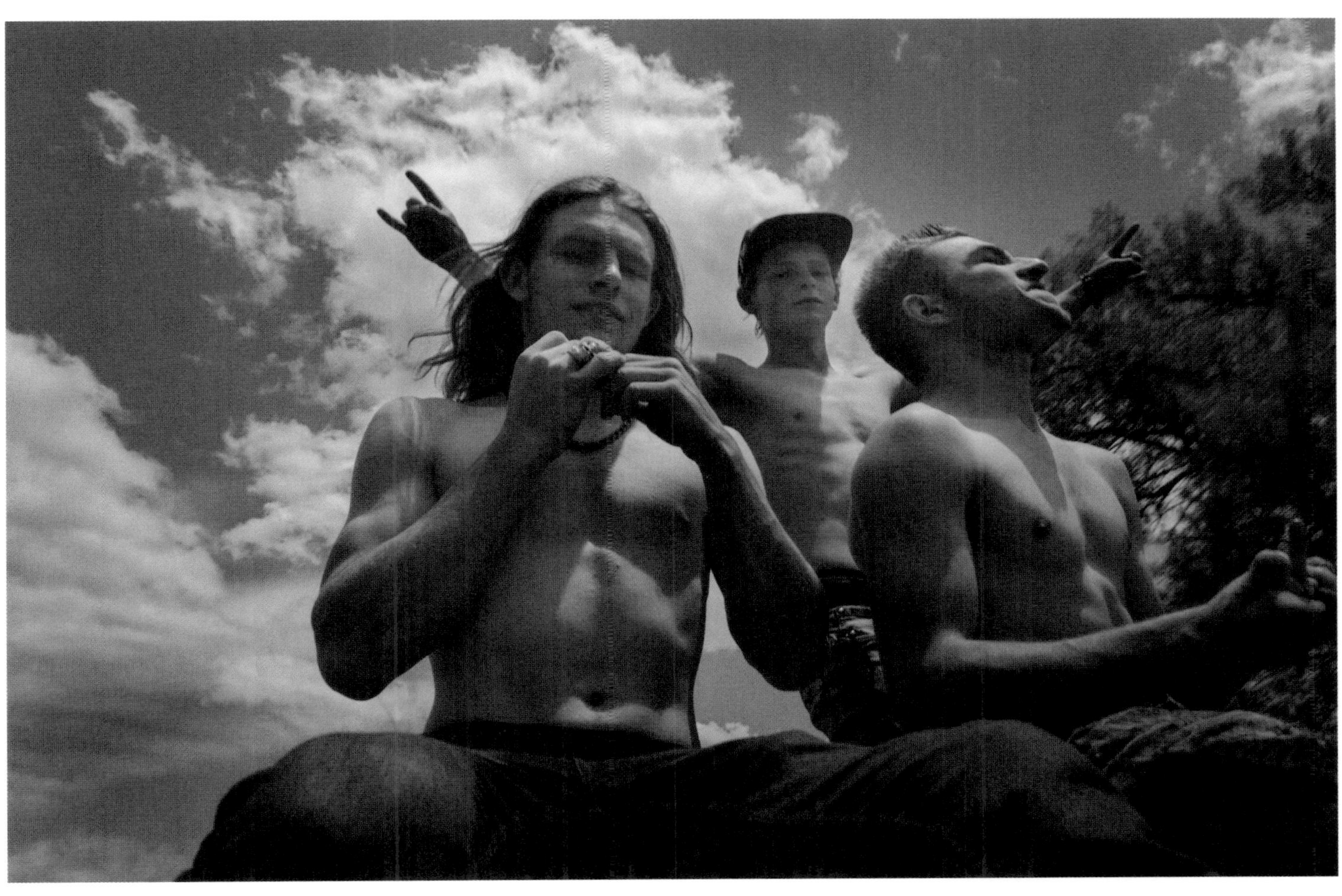

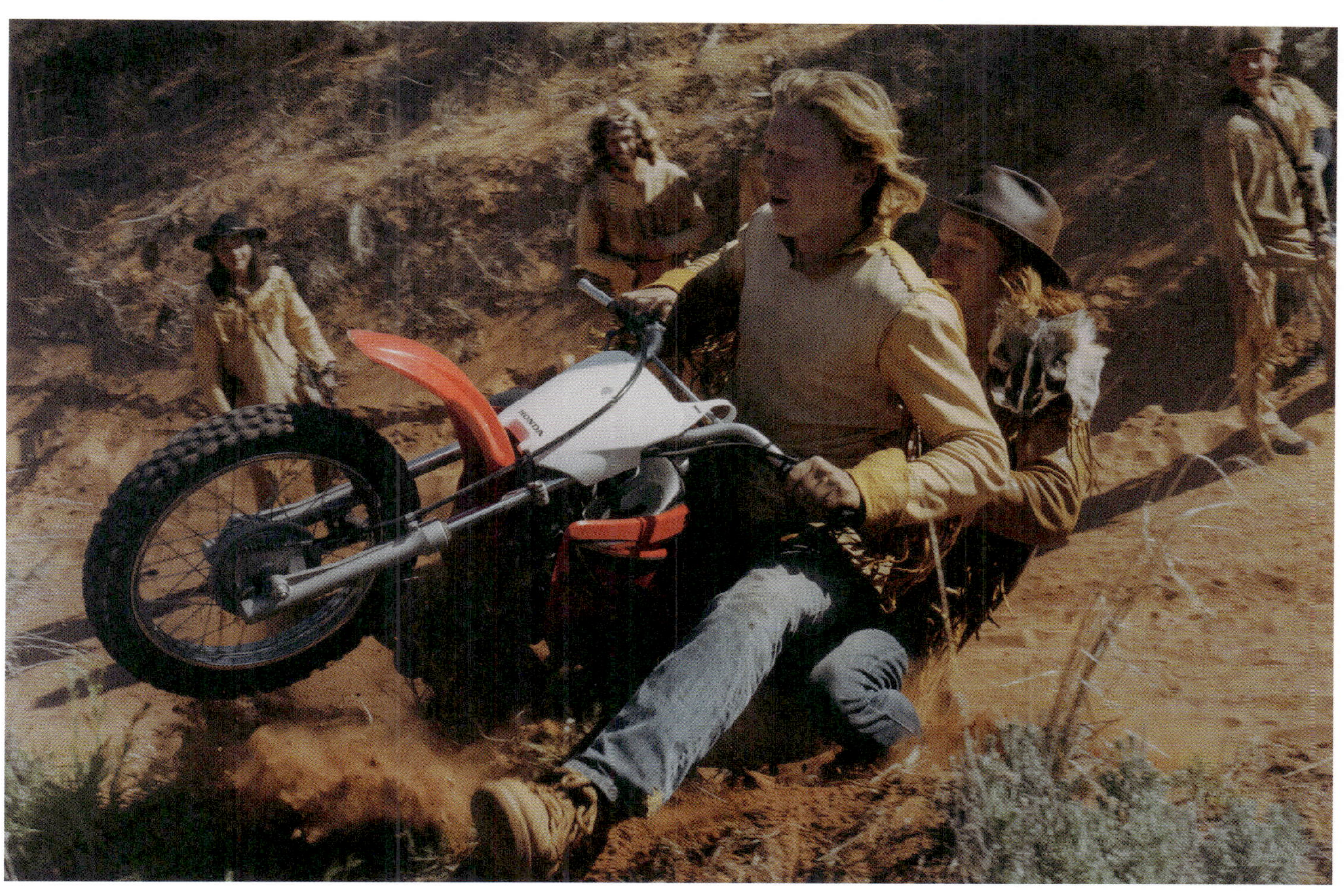
HONDA

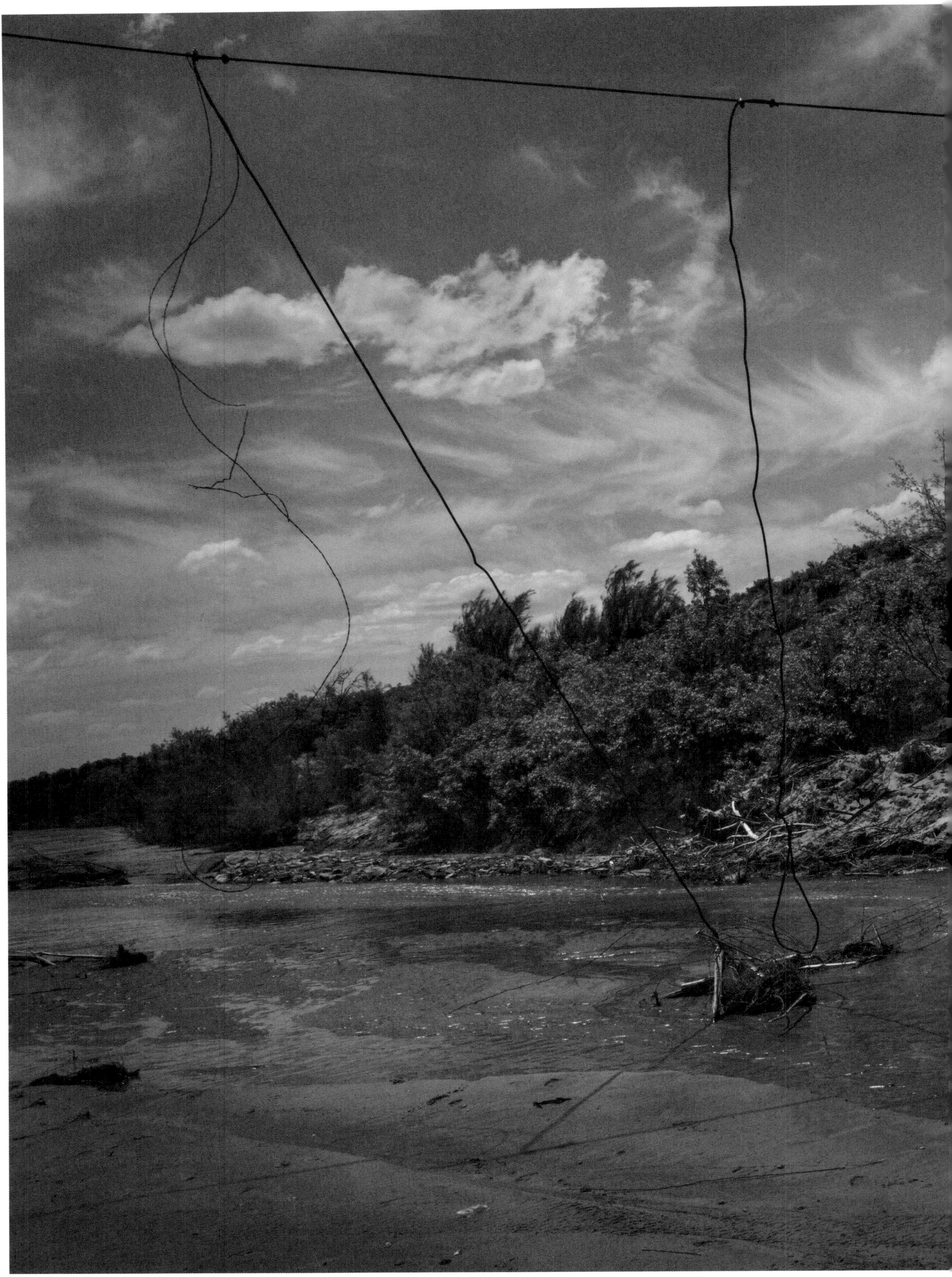

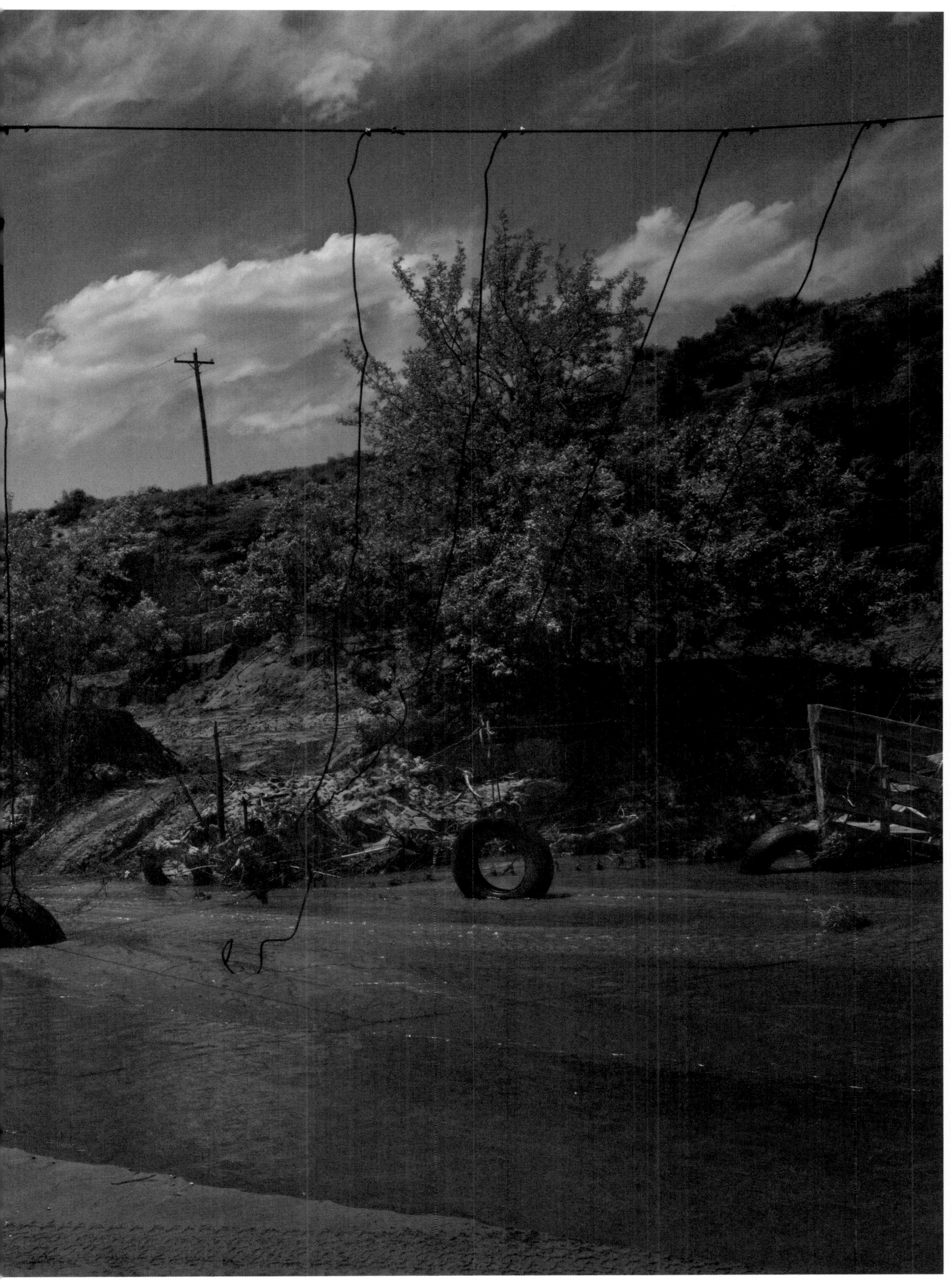

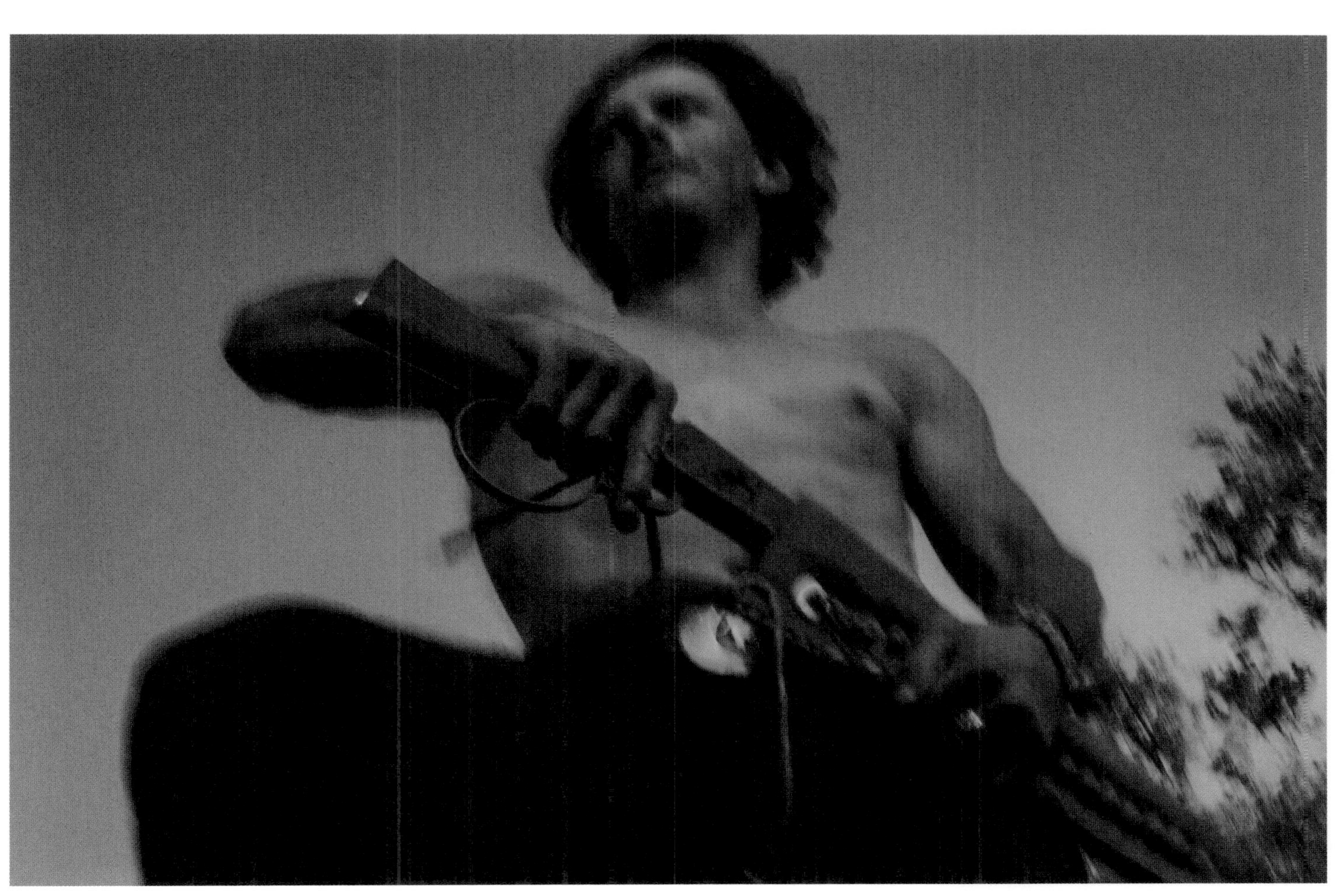

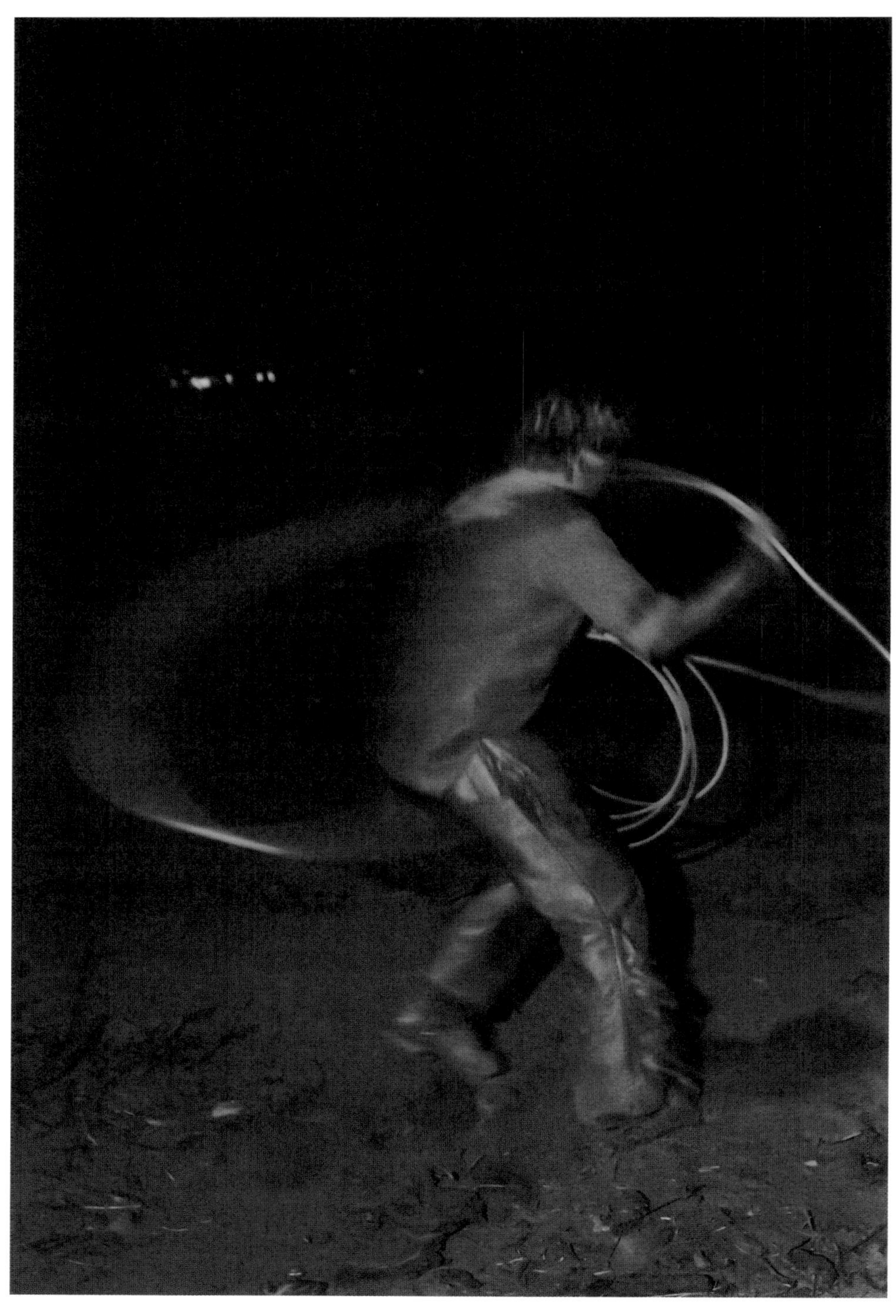

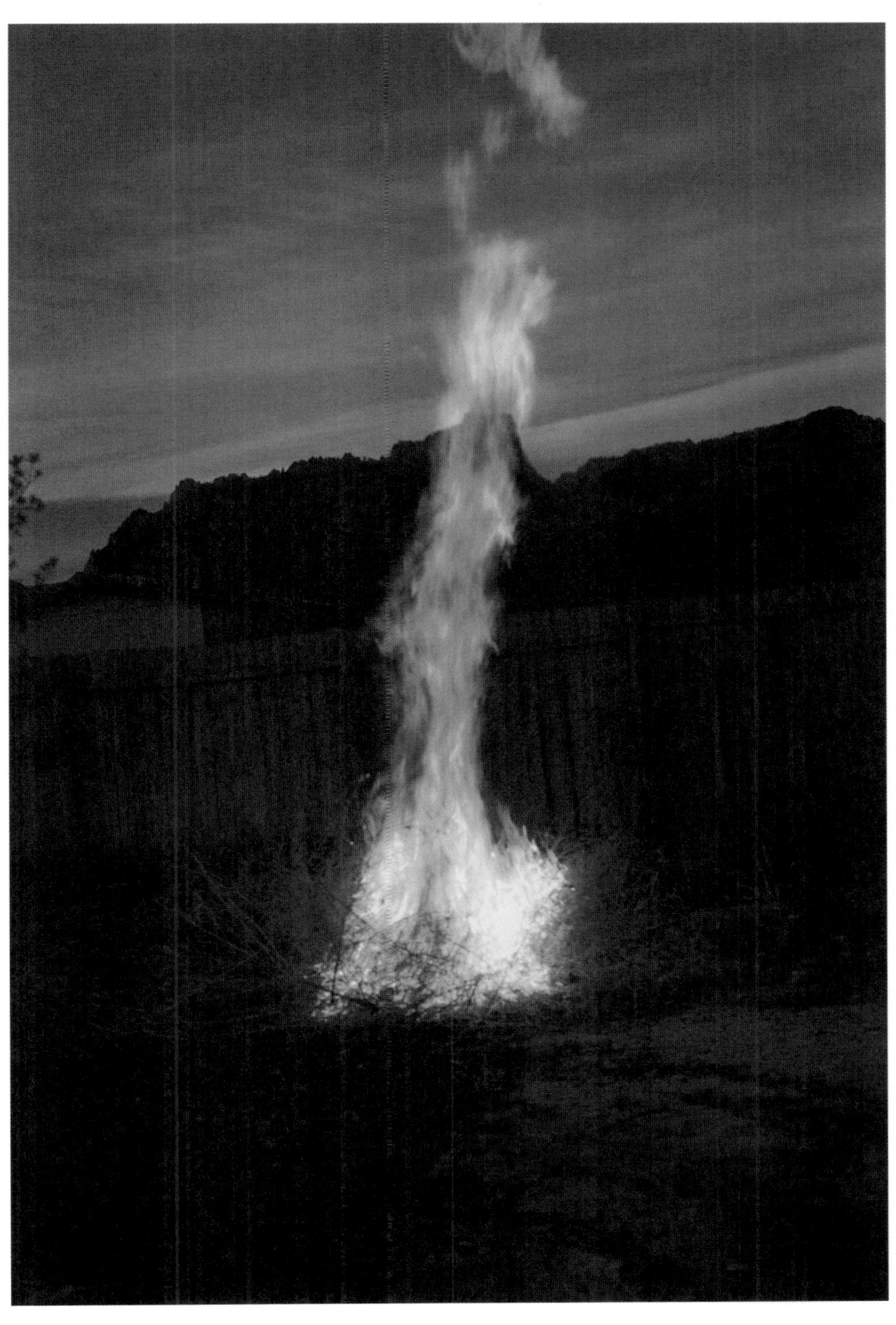

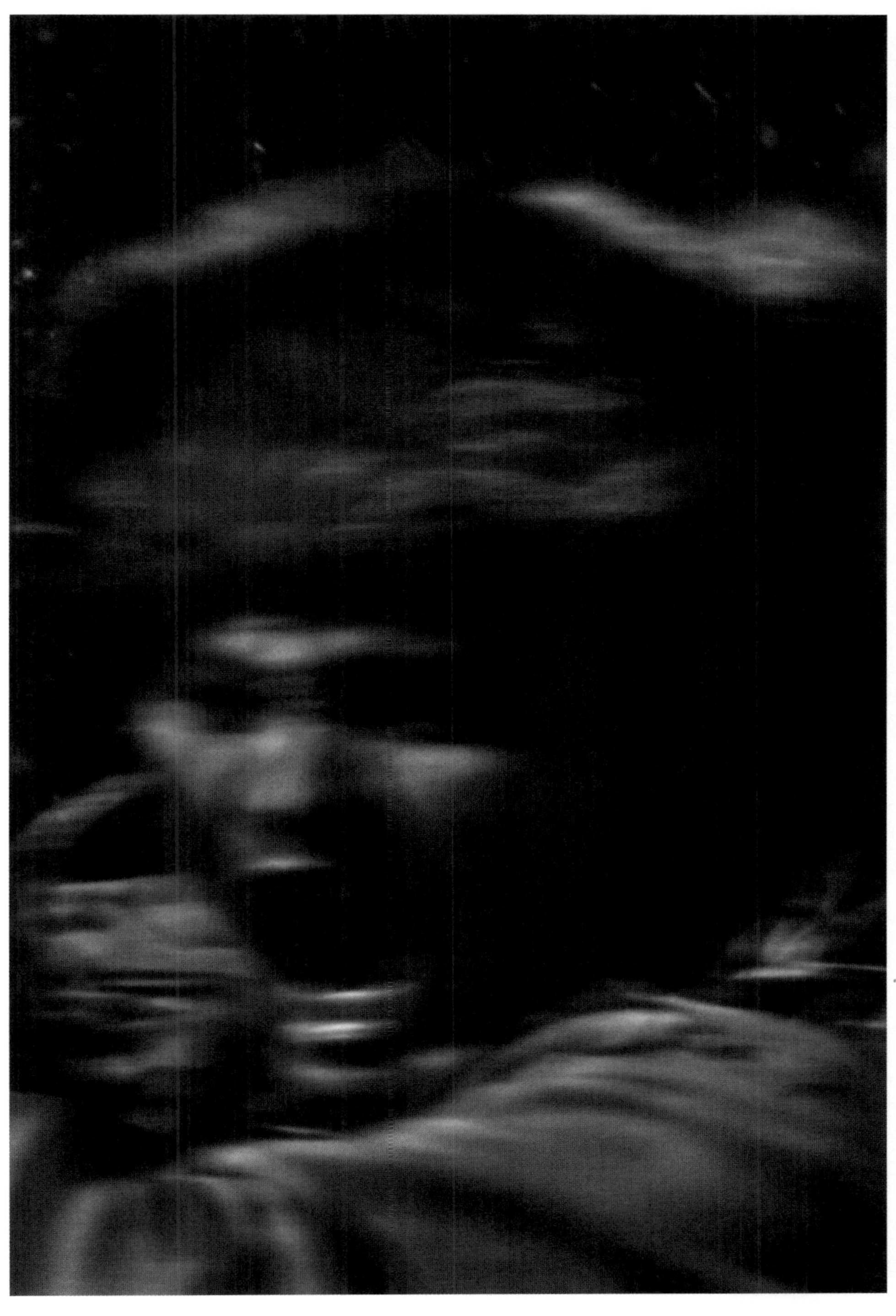

We fill our lungs and the sky with smoke, and dust, and lead, to usher in a dogged red revival. God forbid someone stirs the fucking cesspool.

As children, we and our mothers and father rode alongside the prophet to the pearlied gates of heaven. They were welded shut. It was empty. Then they took our prophet to prison. Our shattered homes and hearts were once again cast hither and yonder like grit in the wind. But some of us boys stayed back with our gnarled beasts and gnarled pedigrees to fill those fucking pearlies with our pistols and ride back to hell where the gates are always wide open.

Born between two worlds, we are
The Lost Lost Boys.

our giants — our stock — our outlaws, they were banished here in the 1800s. The Mormon Church had signed a manifesto forbidding the practice of polygamy. Our giants, our stock, our outlaws, they spurned righteously. Then they and their posterity were cast hither and yonder like grit in the wind. Some died frozen to the ground. Some fell filled with lead, others with arrows. Some dried up and blew away. Most were exiled to this desert — to the fringes of hell where all is legal and the fatal sun hangs hot, and high, and heavy.

Then it plunges and hell freezes over. It's God's country, although he vacated long ago, leaving it to the clever or reptilian, leaving it to us trigger happy lovers, to us trigger happy sinners and with our righteous indignation we fill our riotous hearts and horses with gasoline.

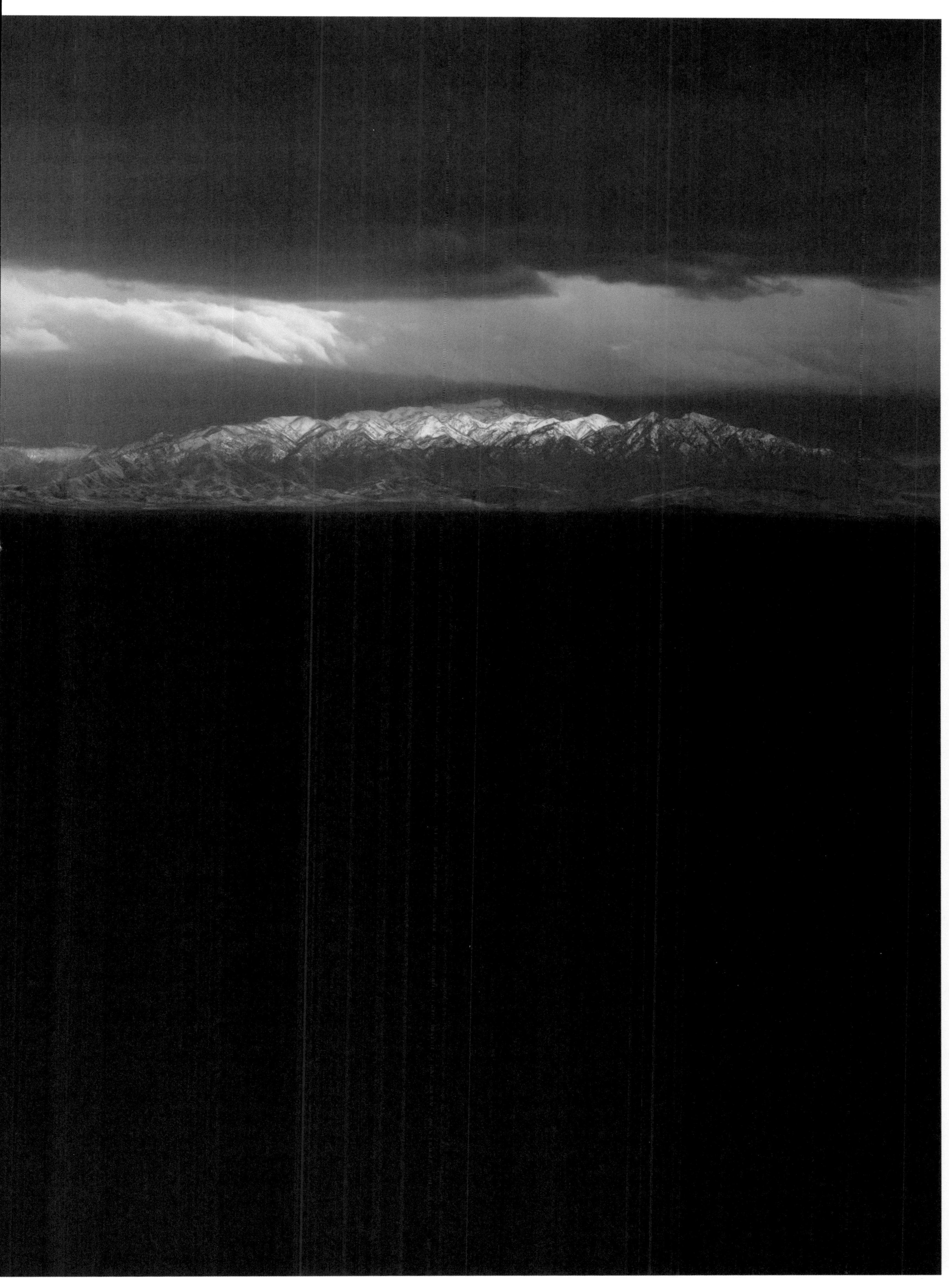

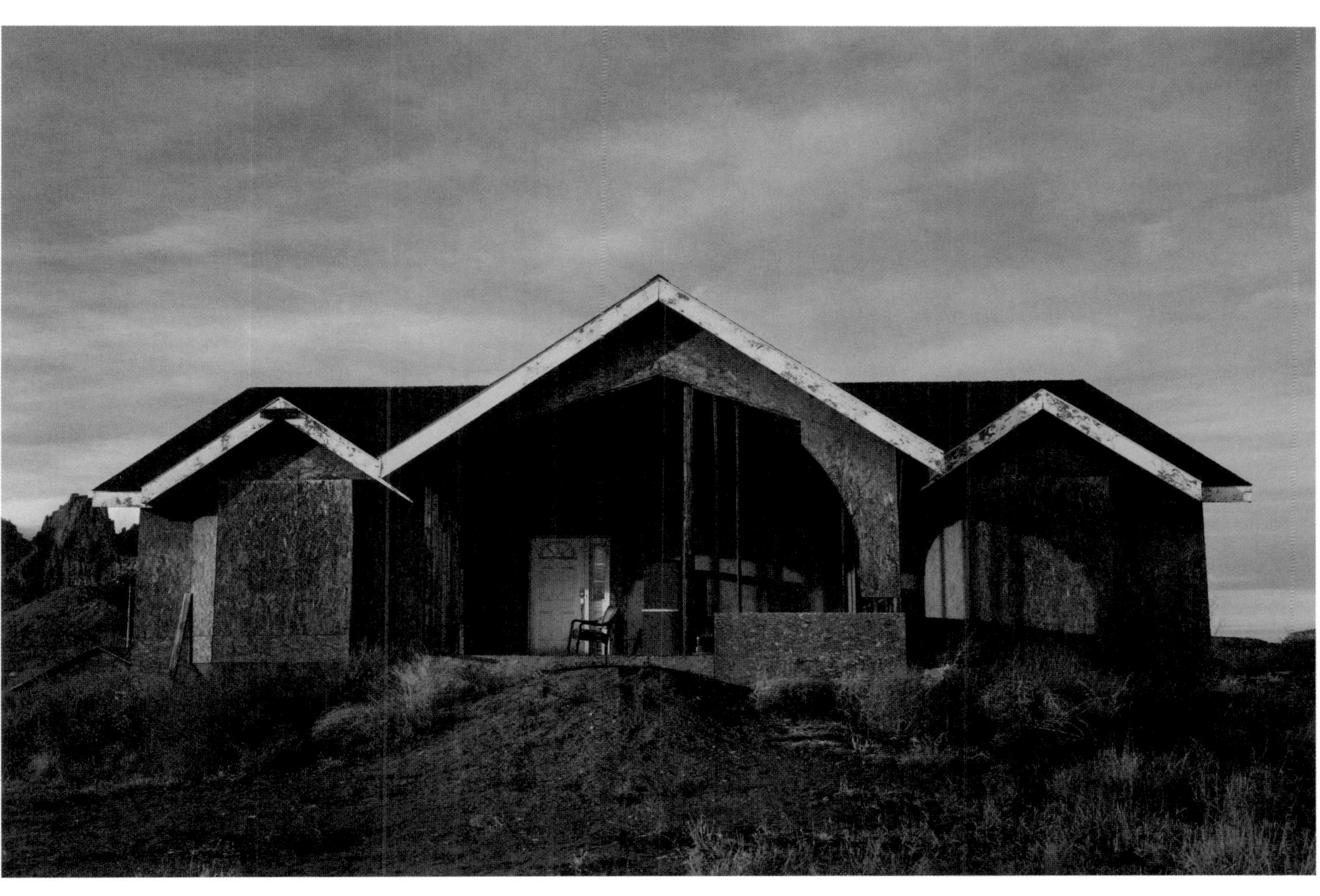

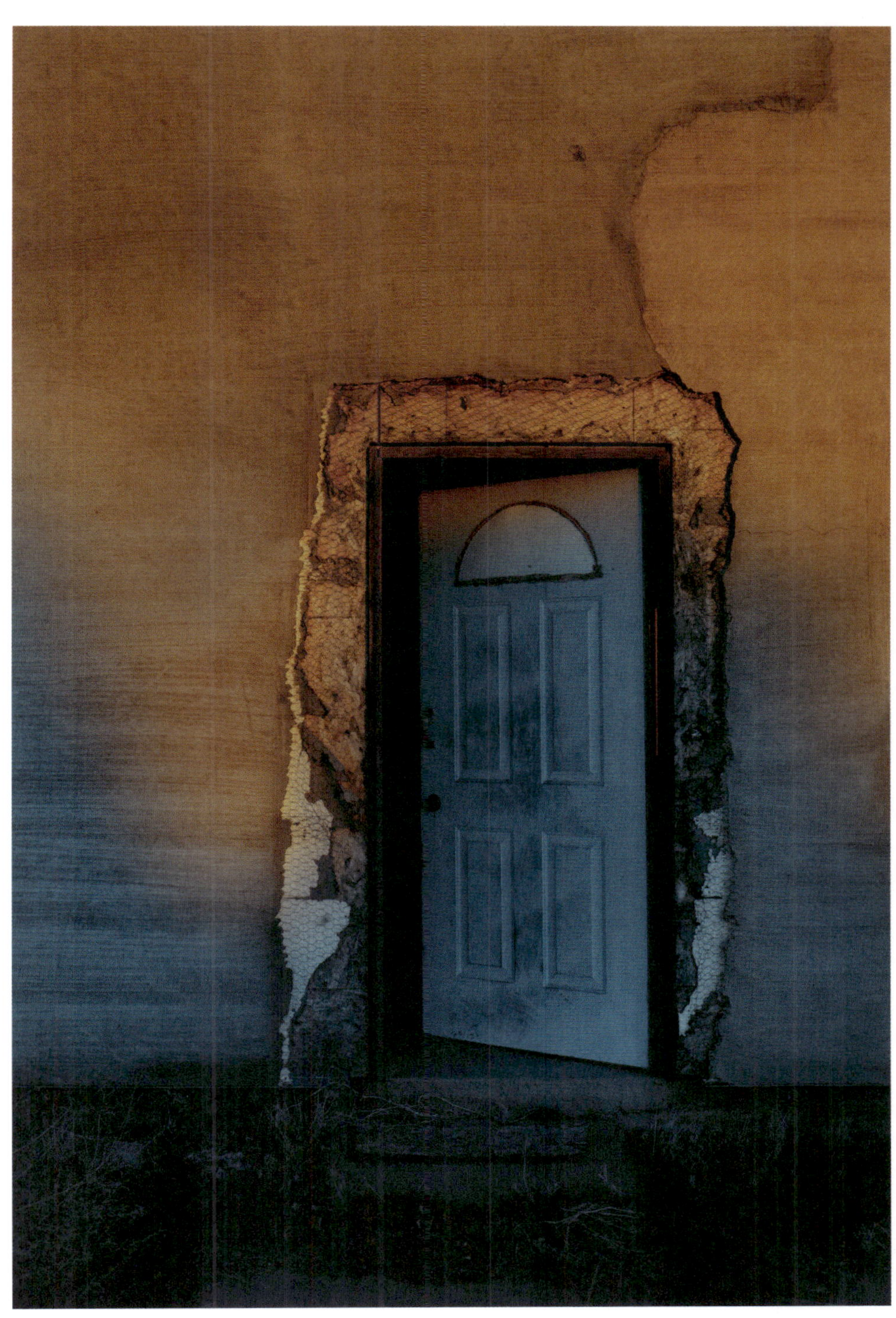

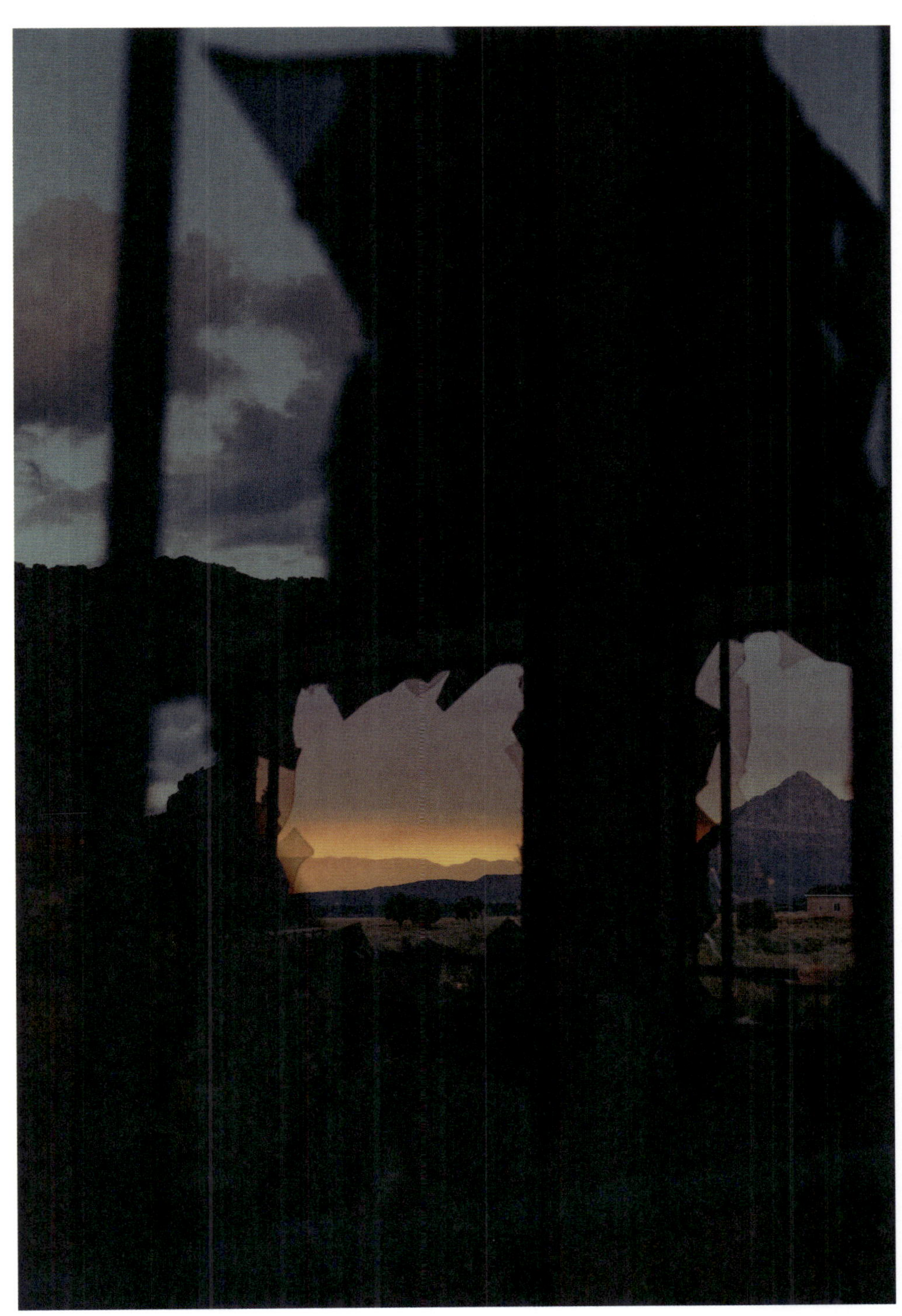

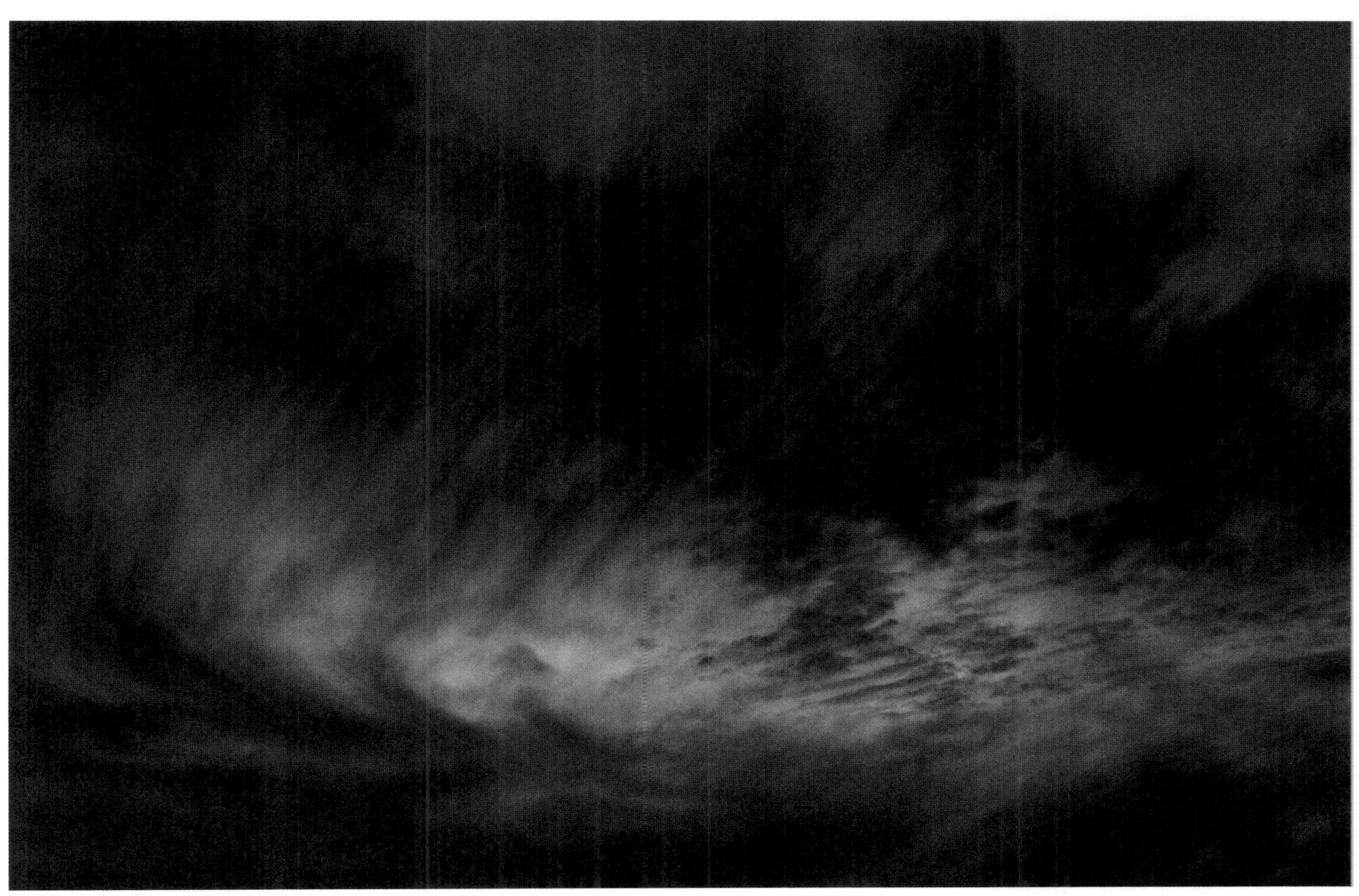

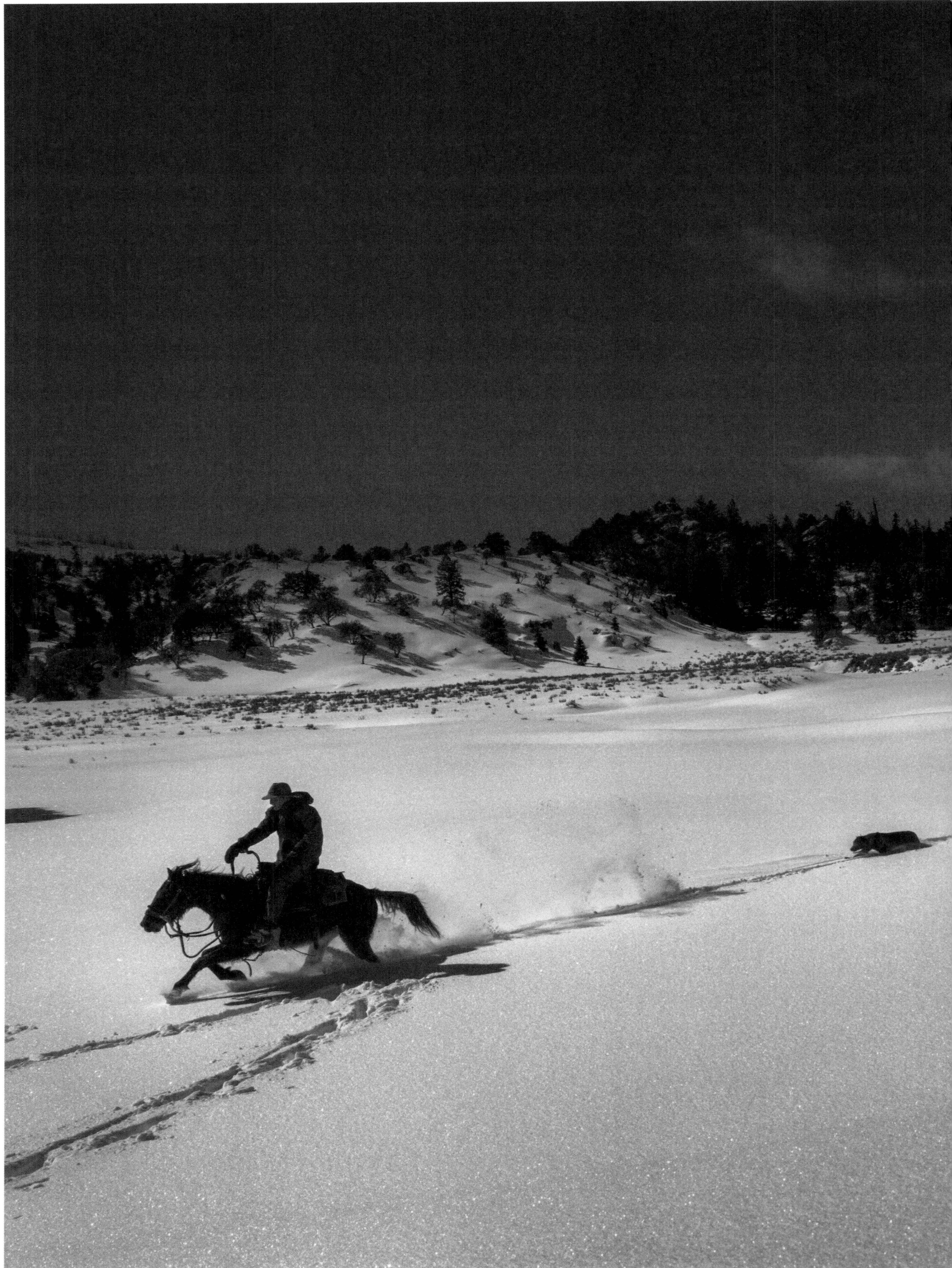

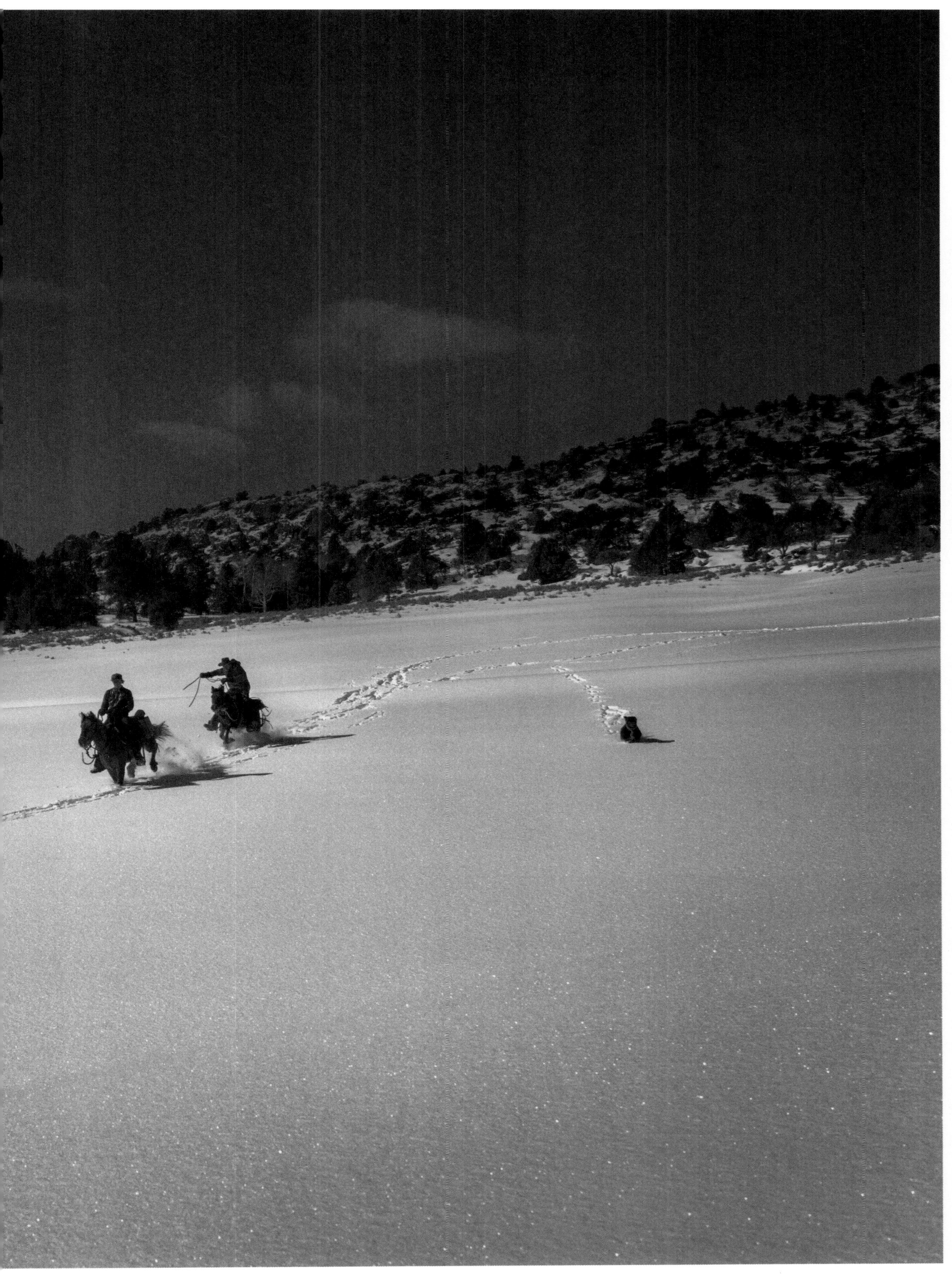

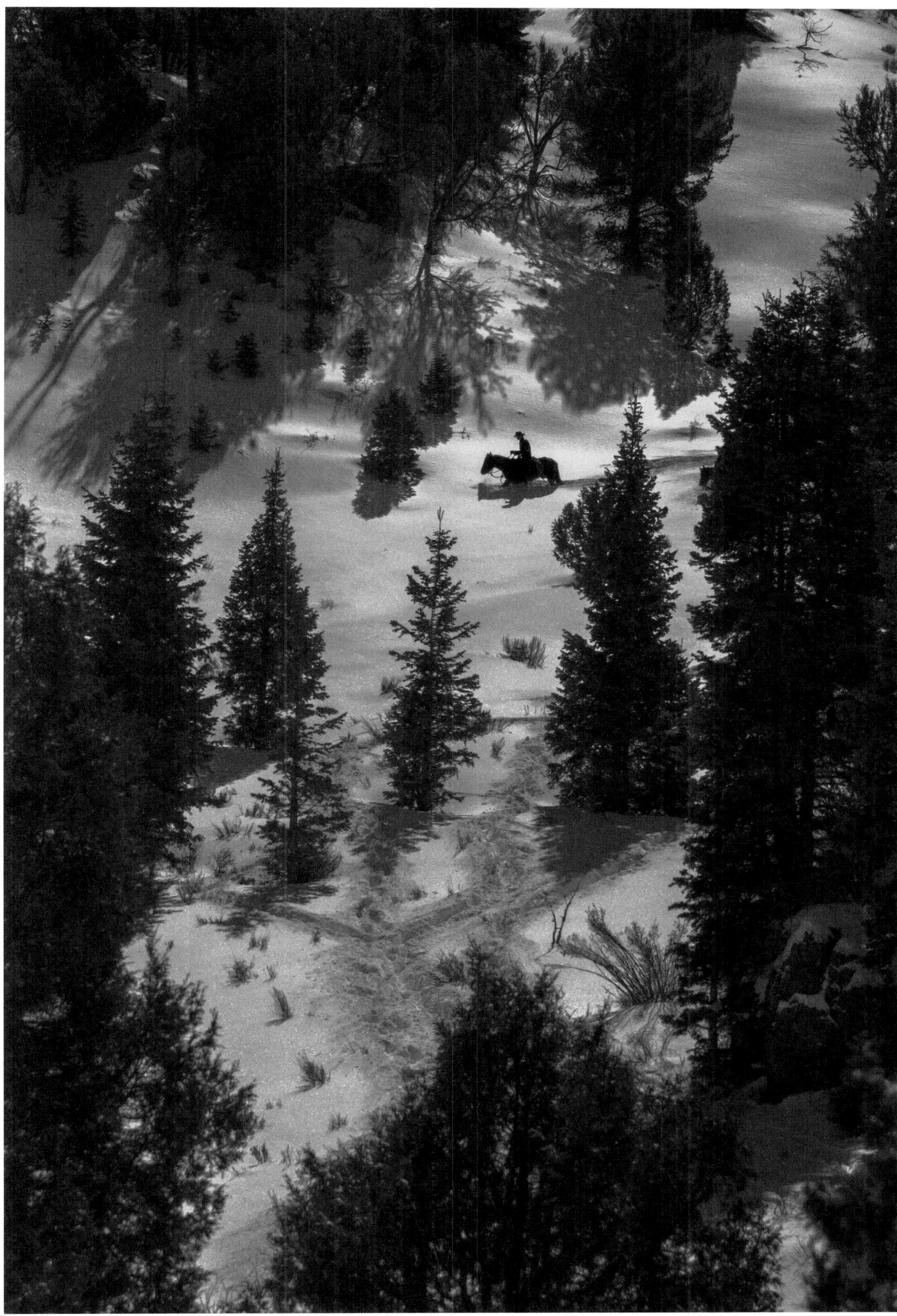

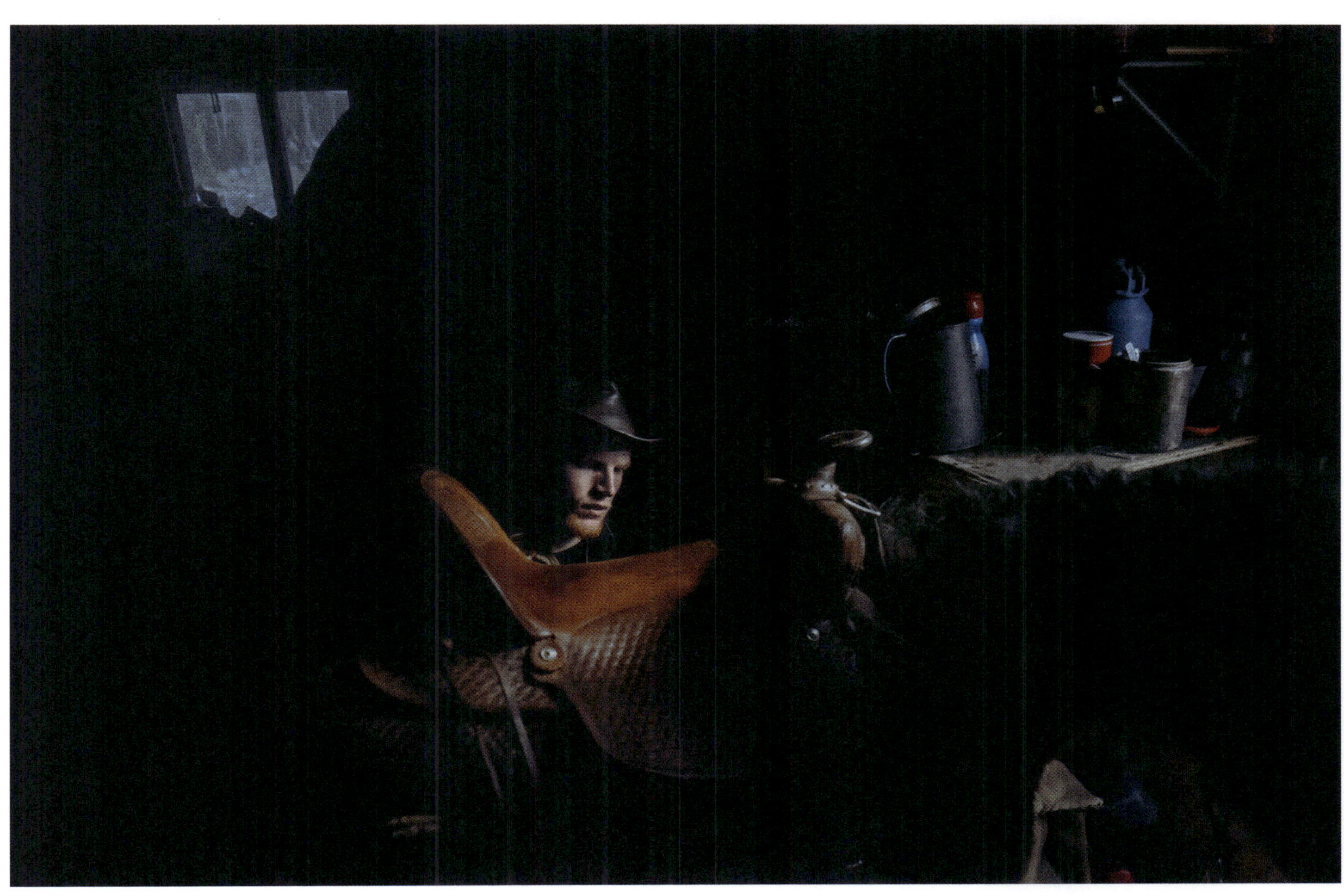

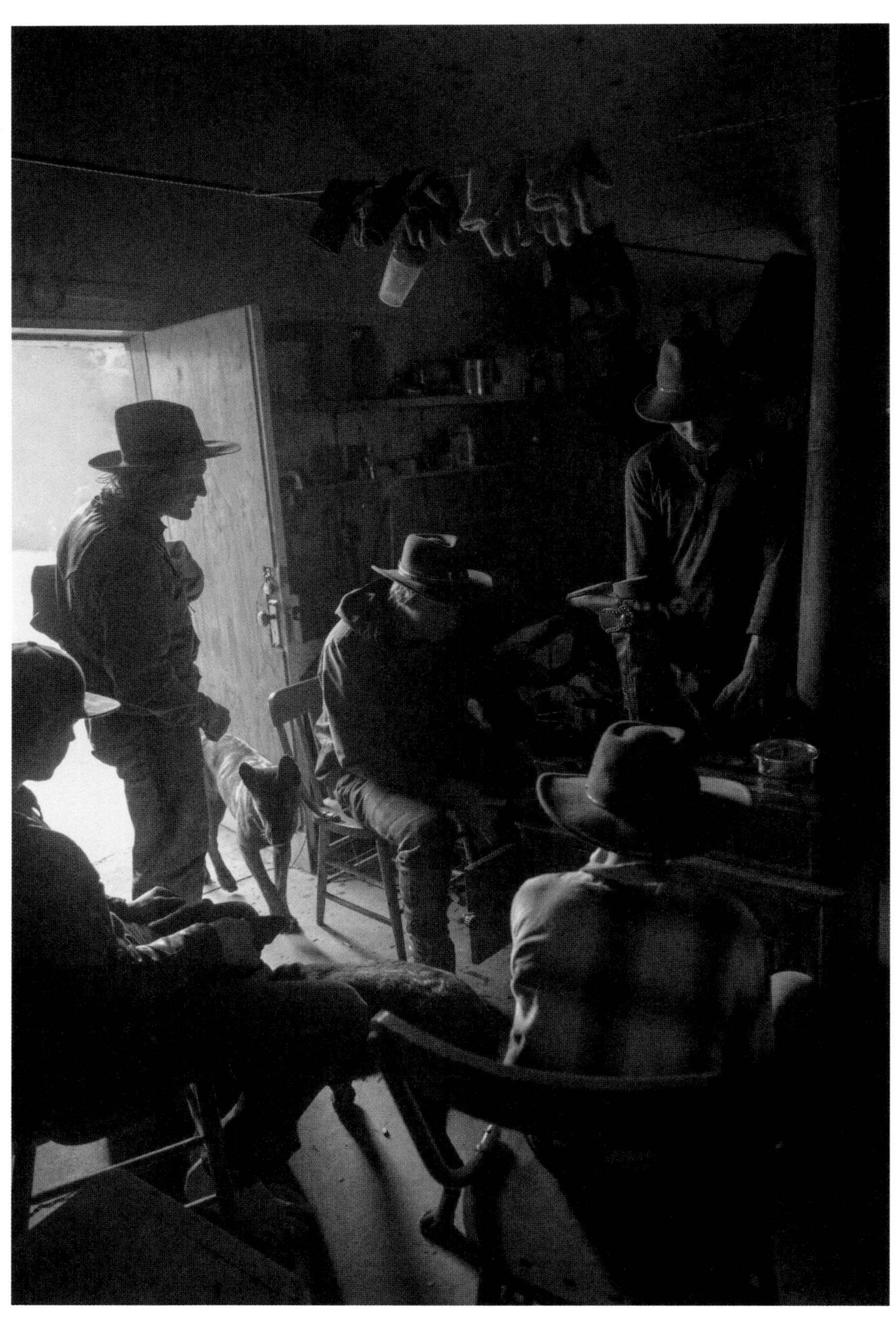

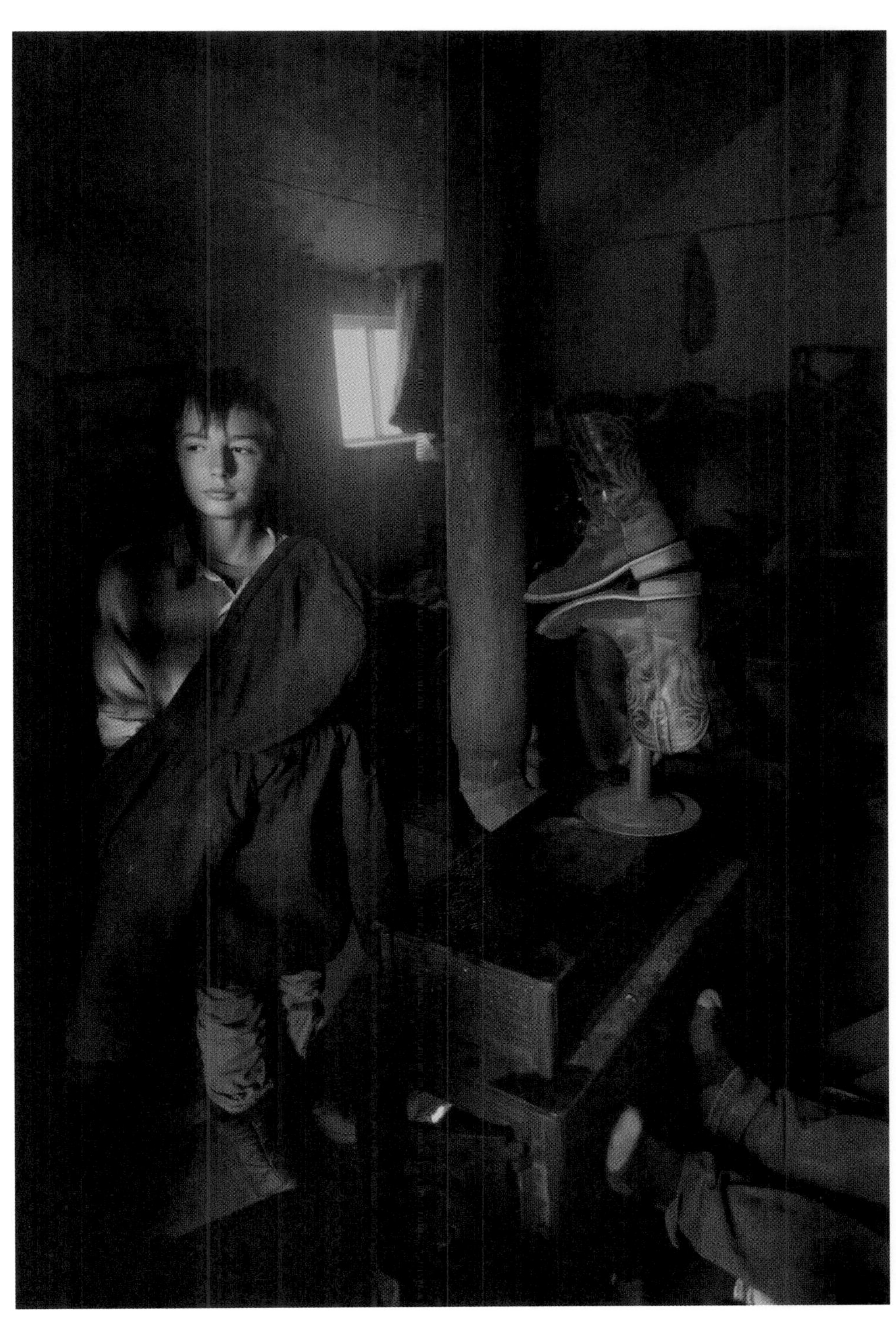

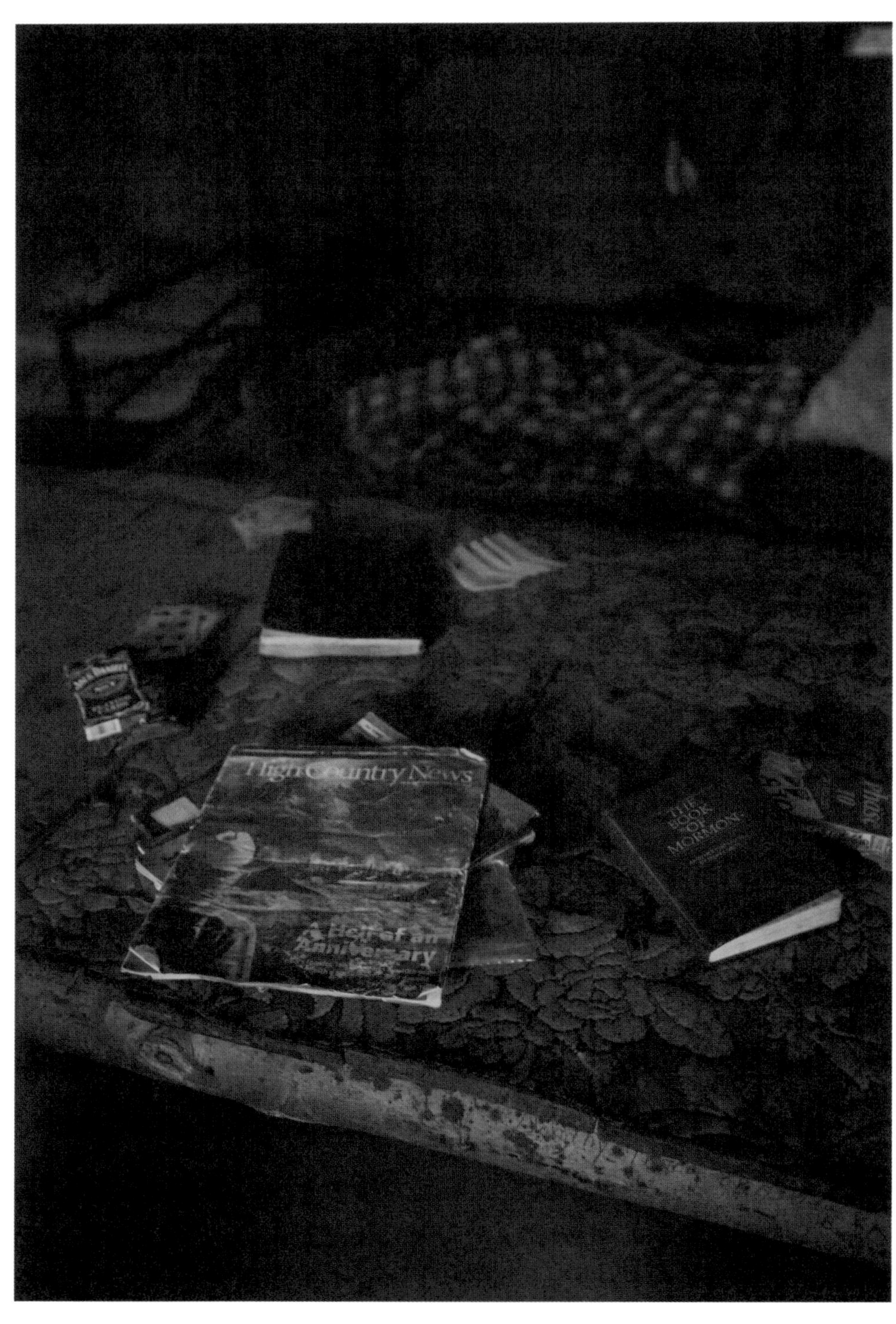
High Country News
THE BOOK OF MORMON

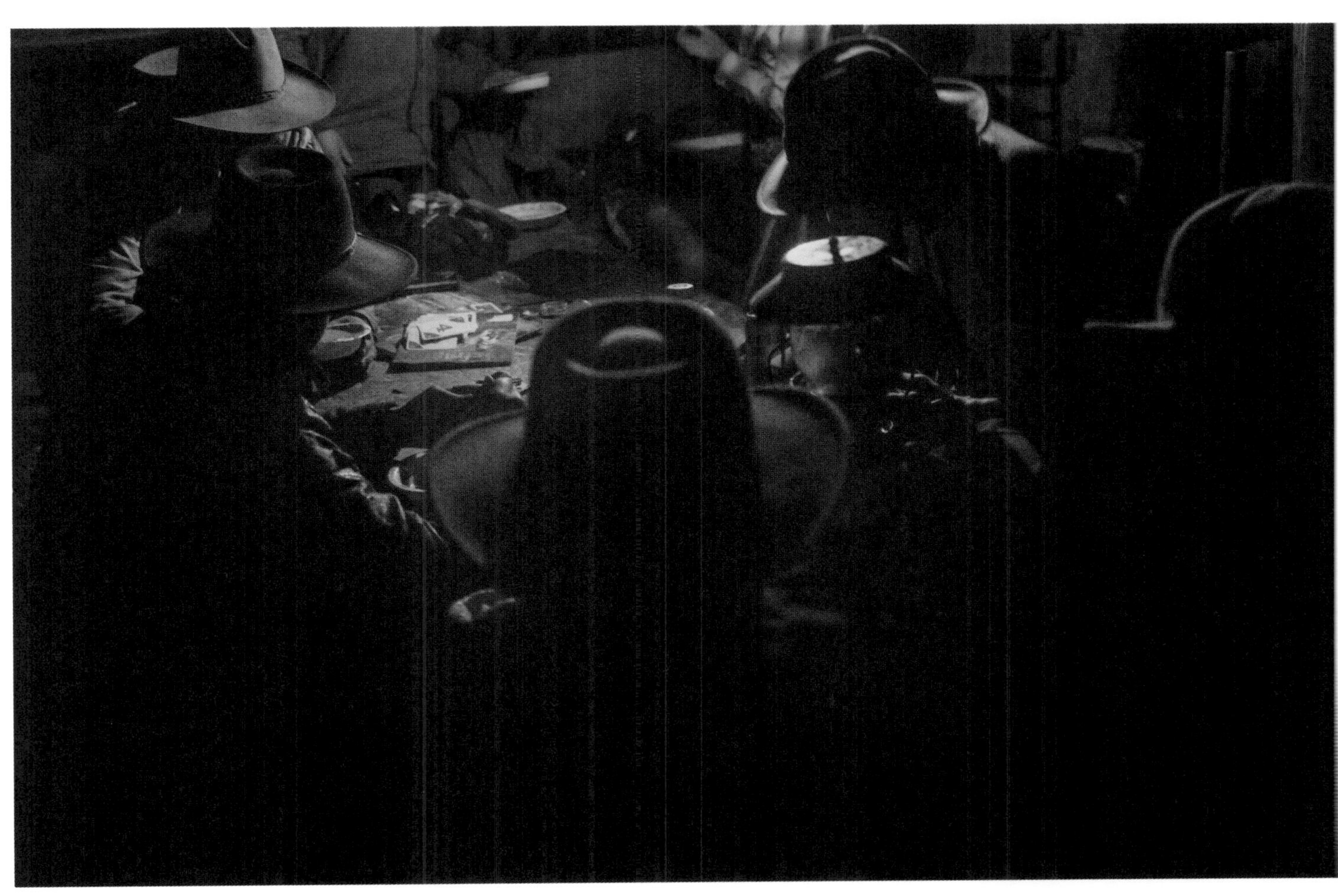

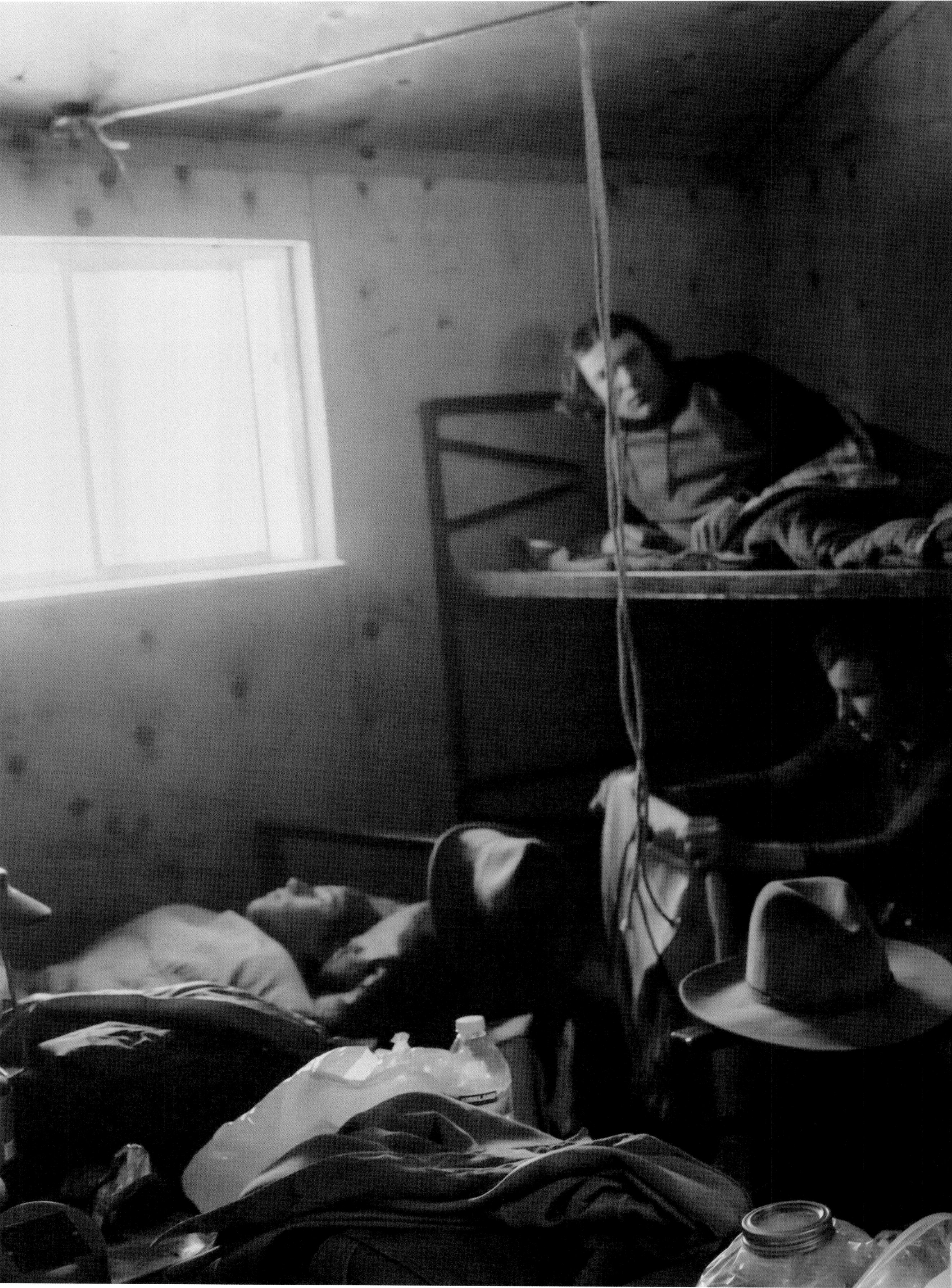

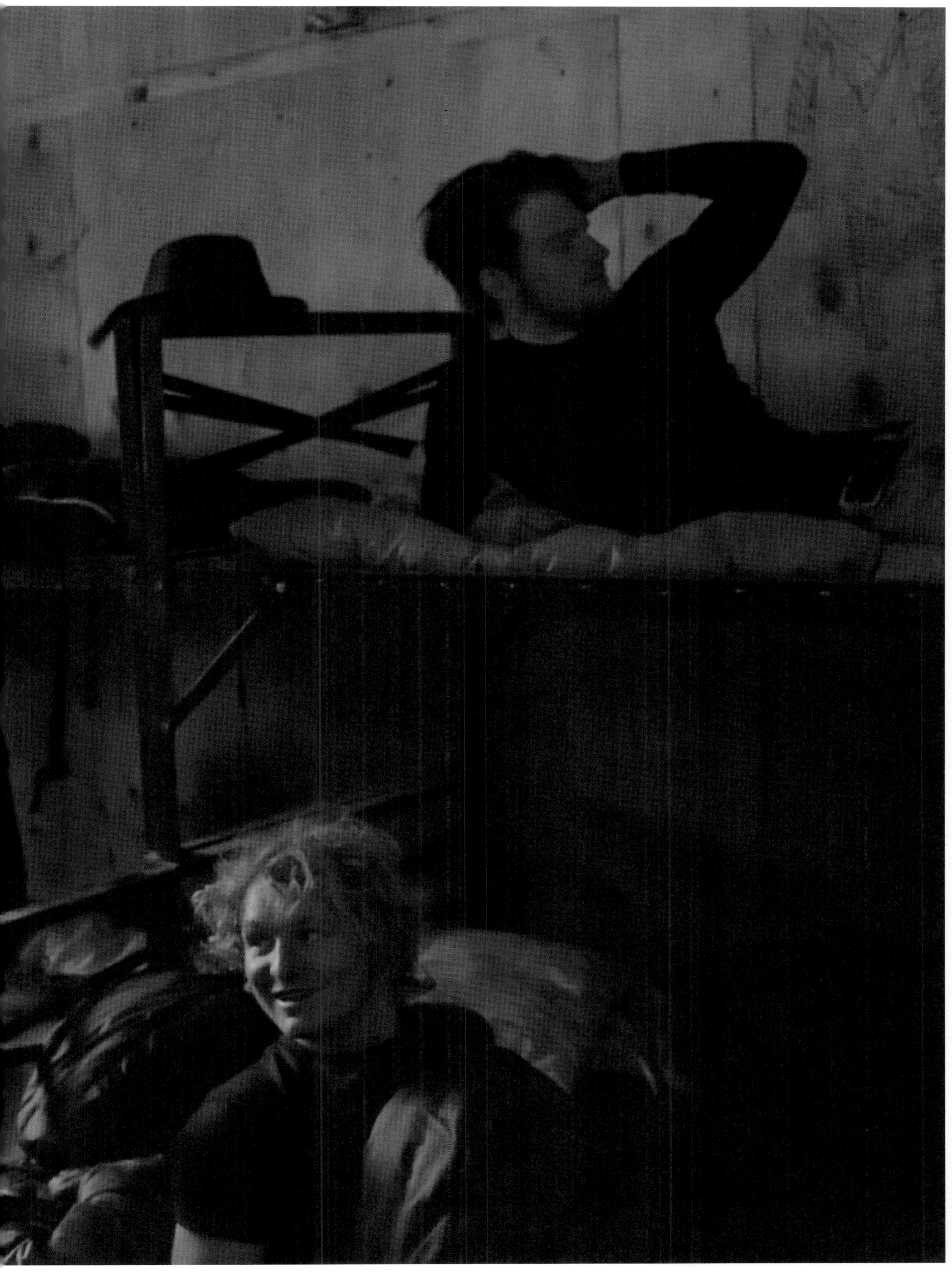

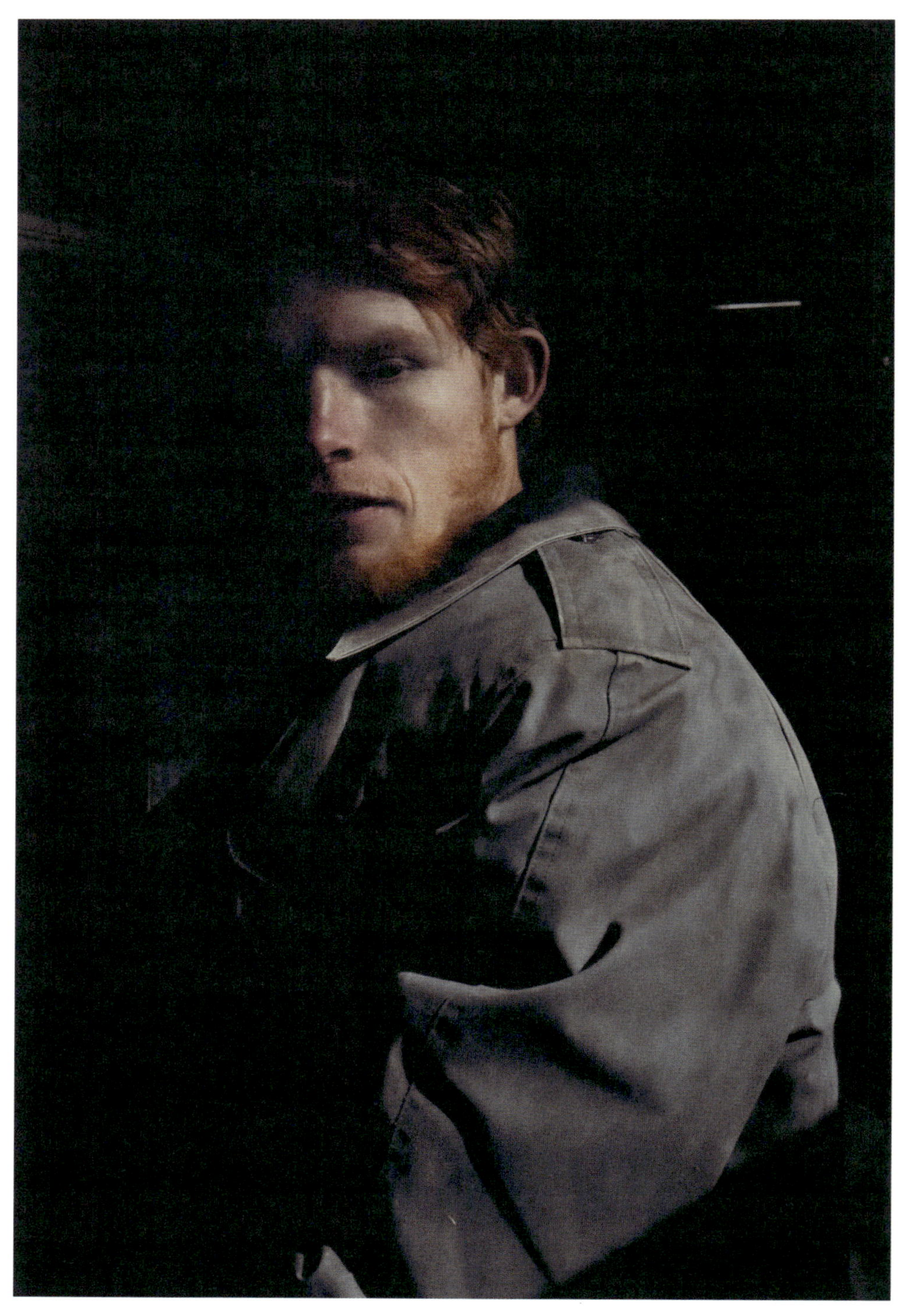

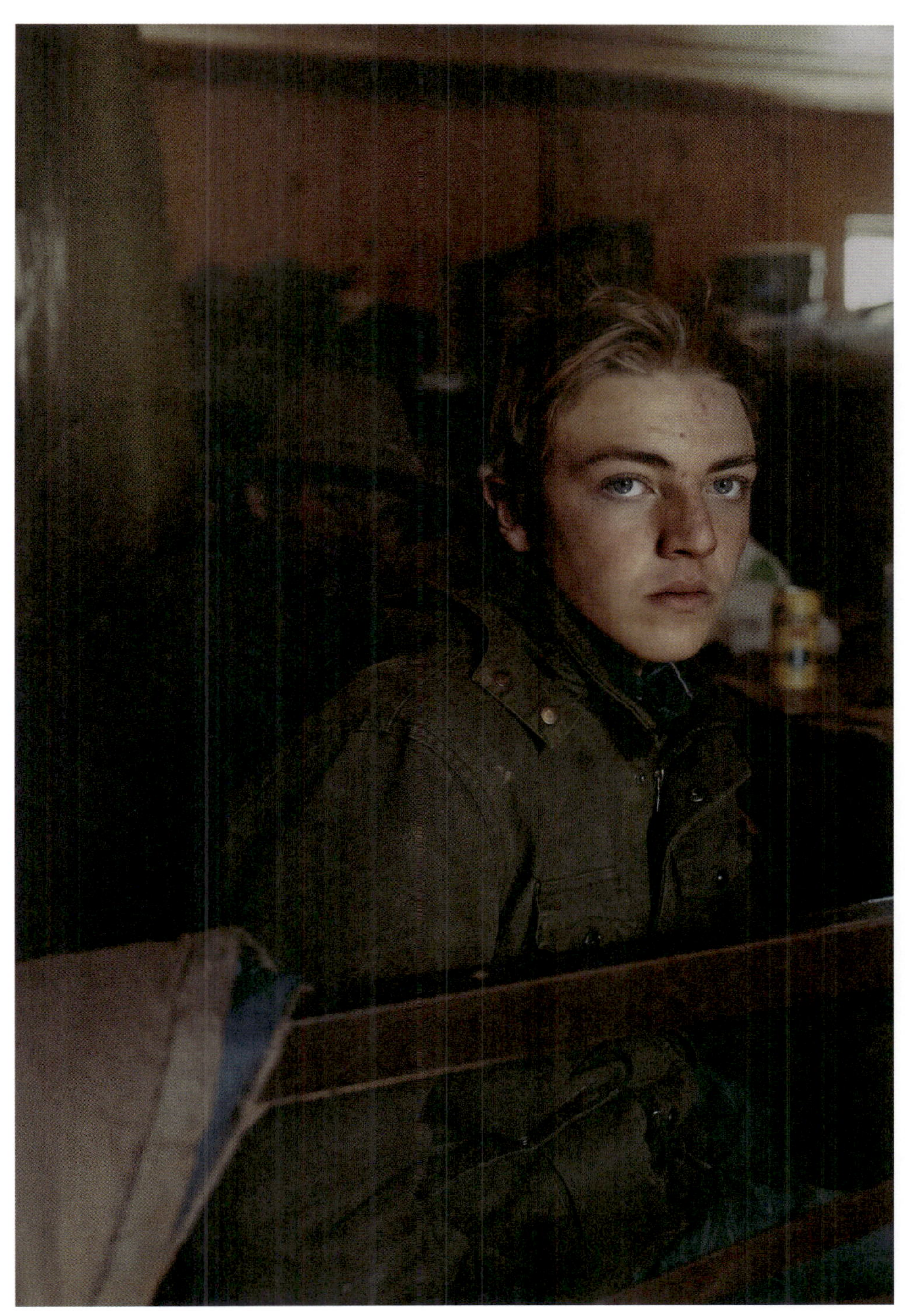

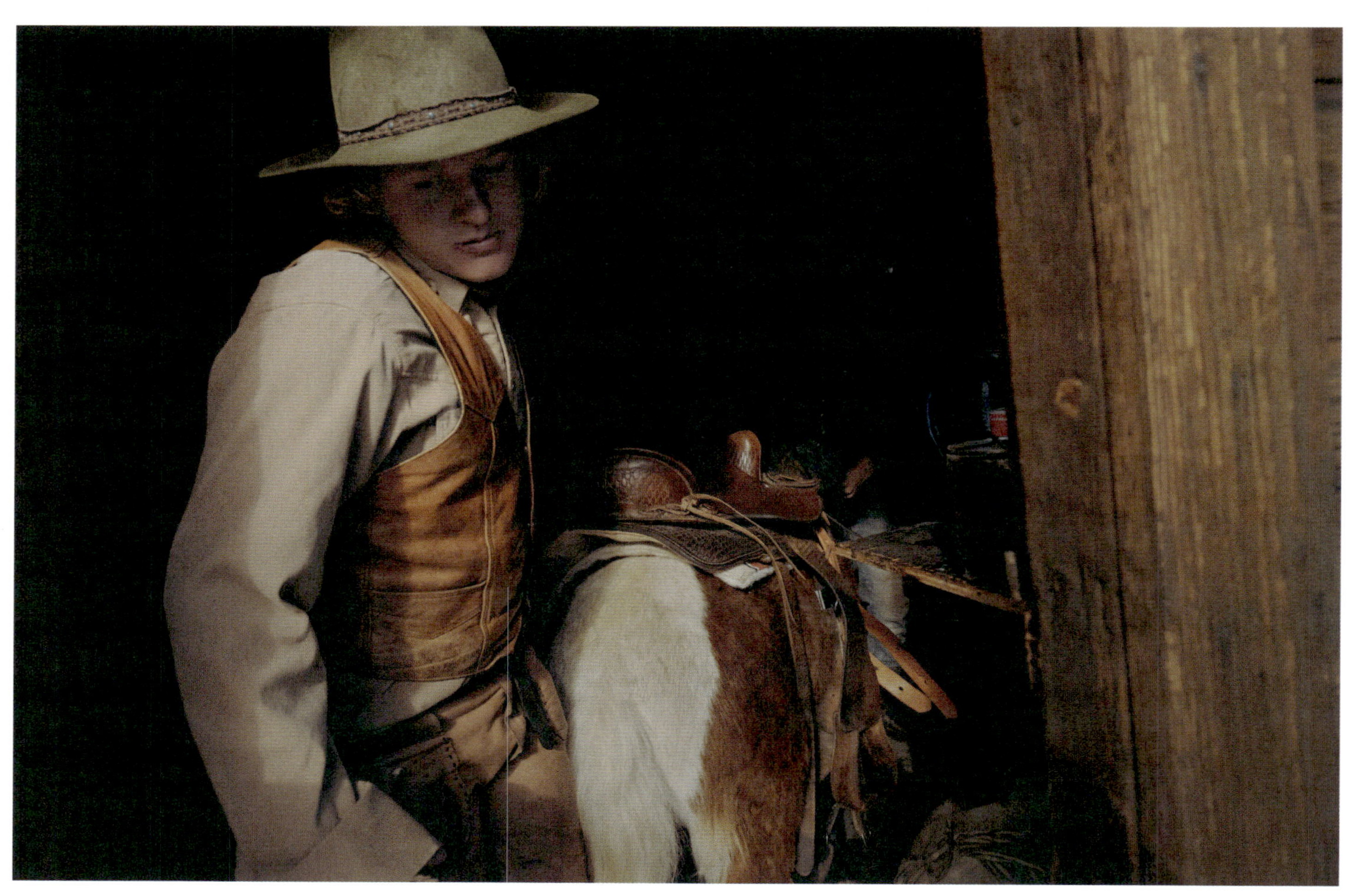

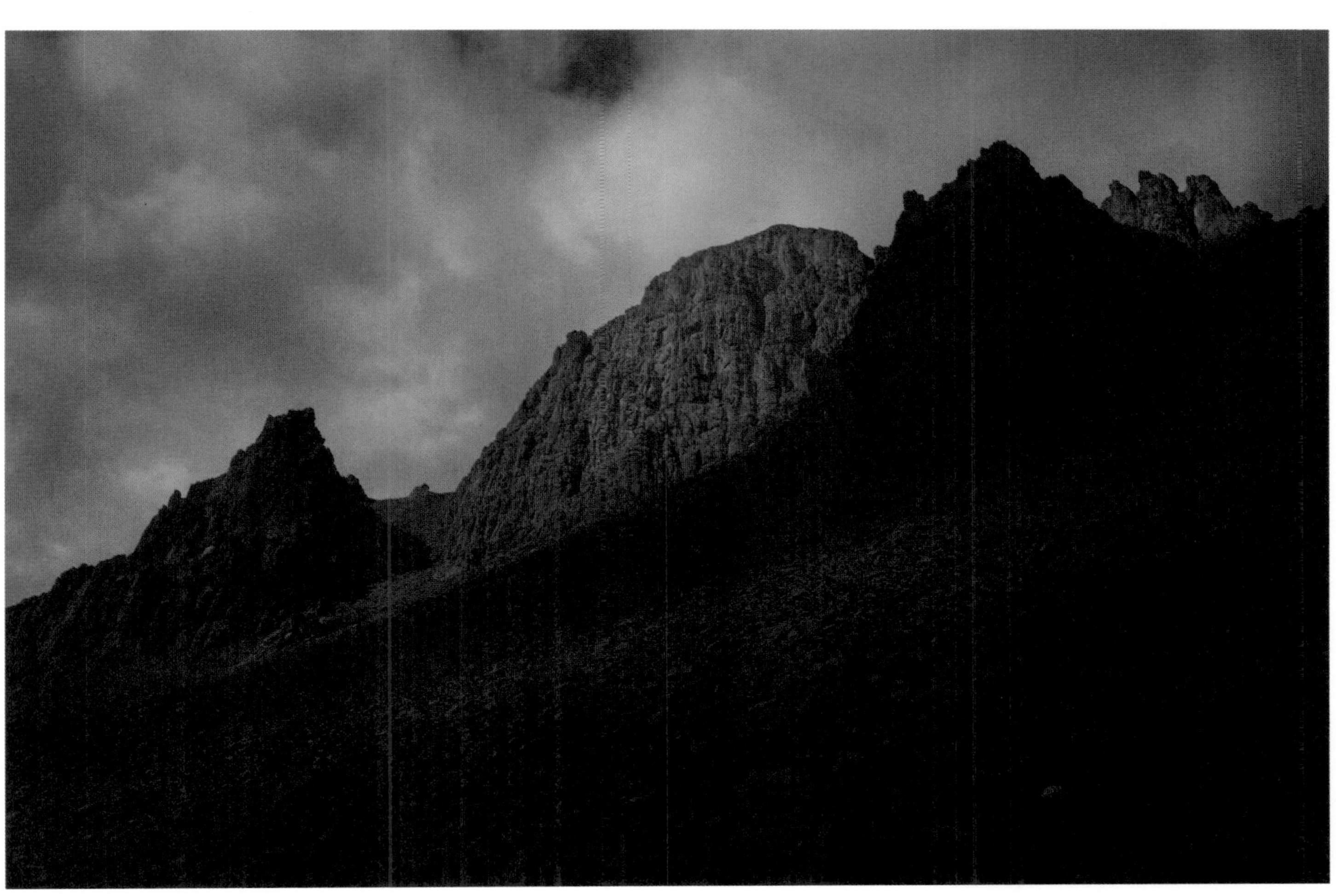

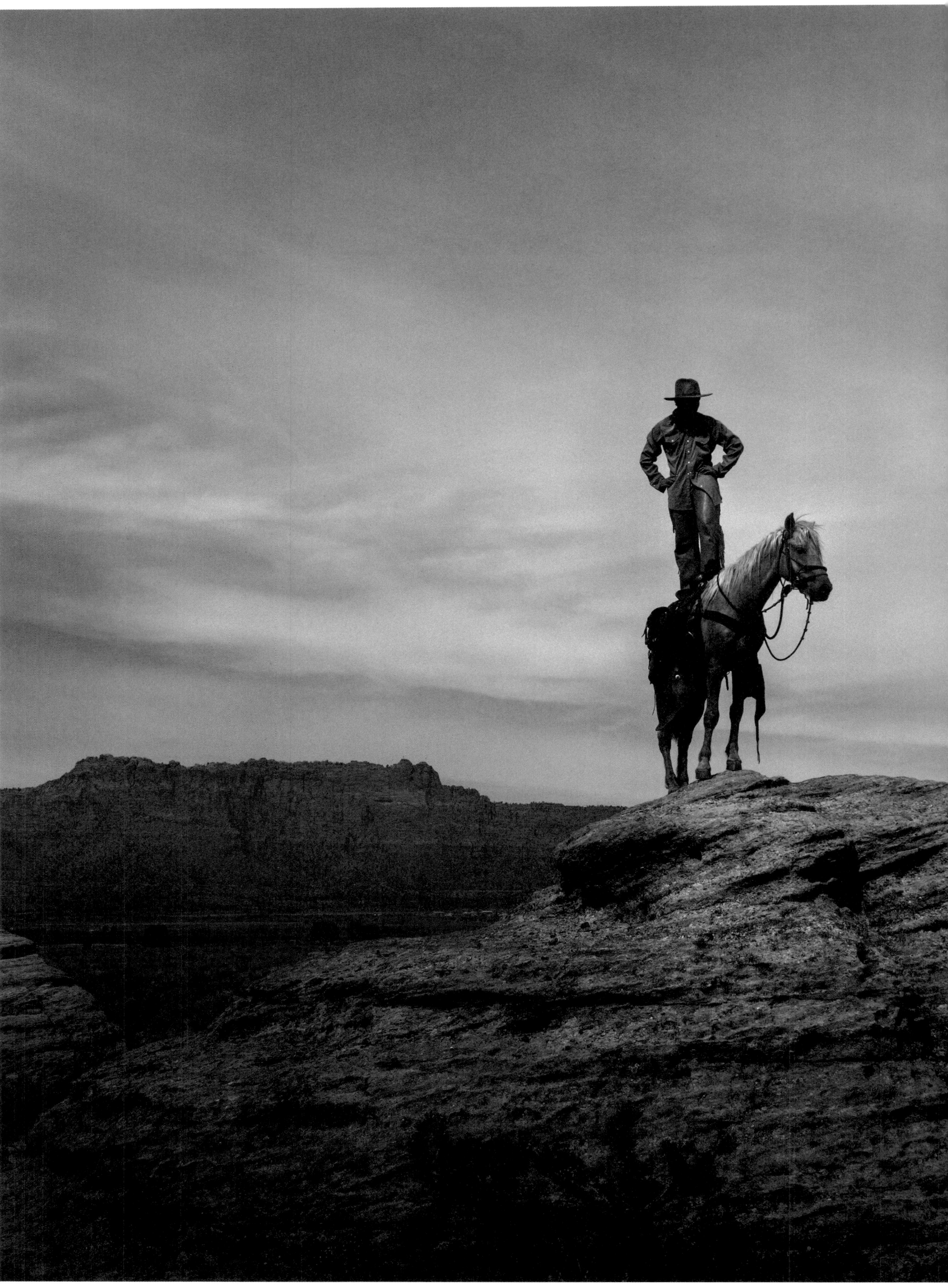

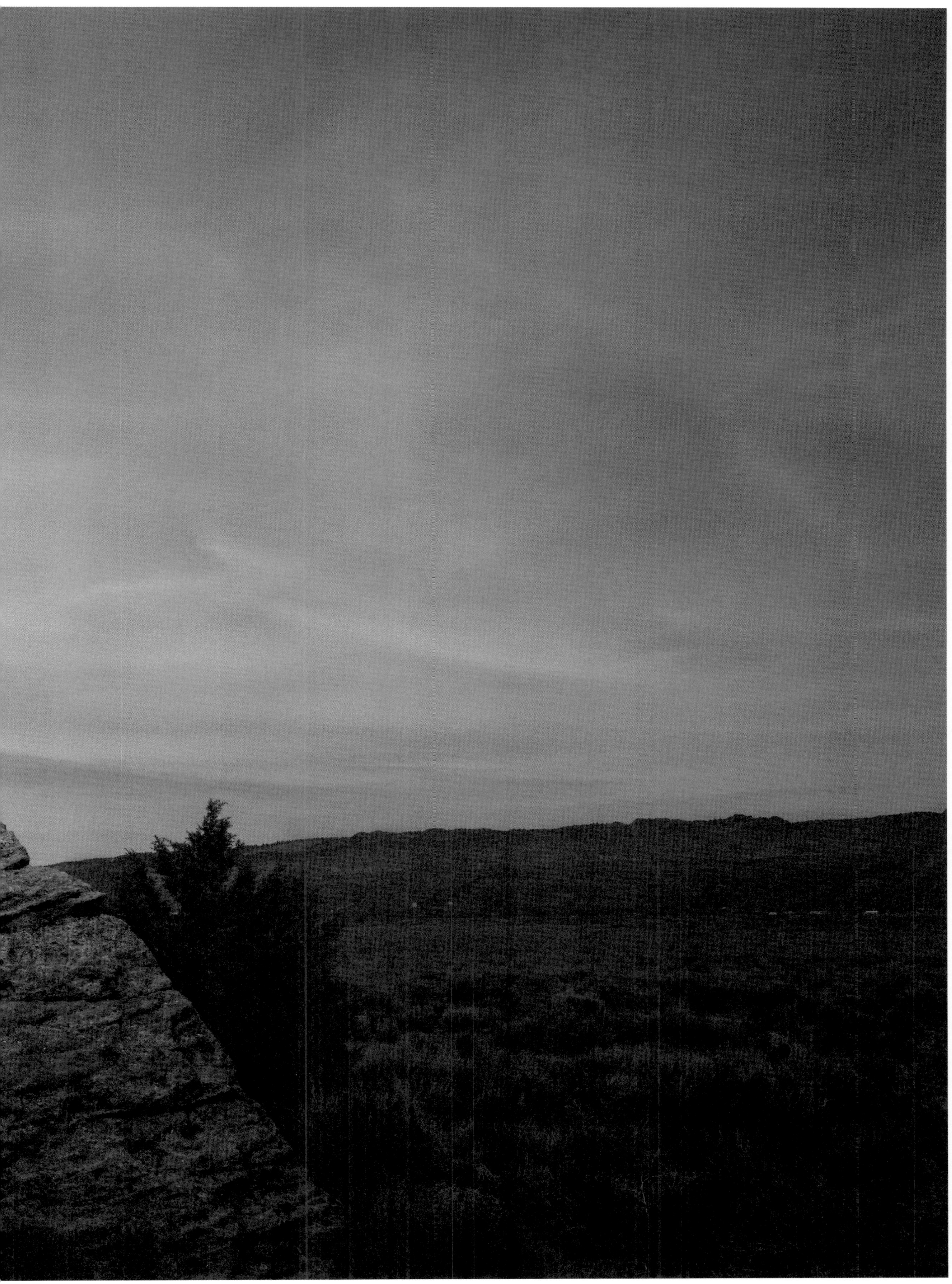

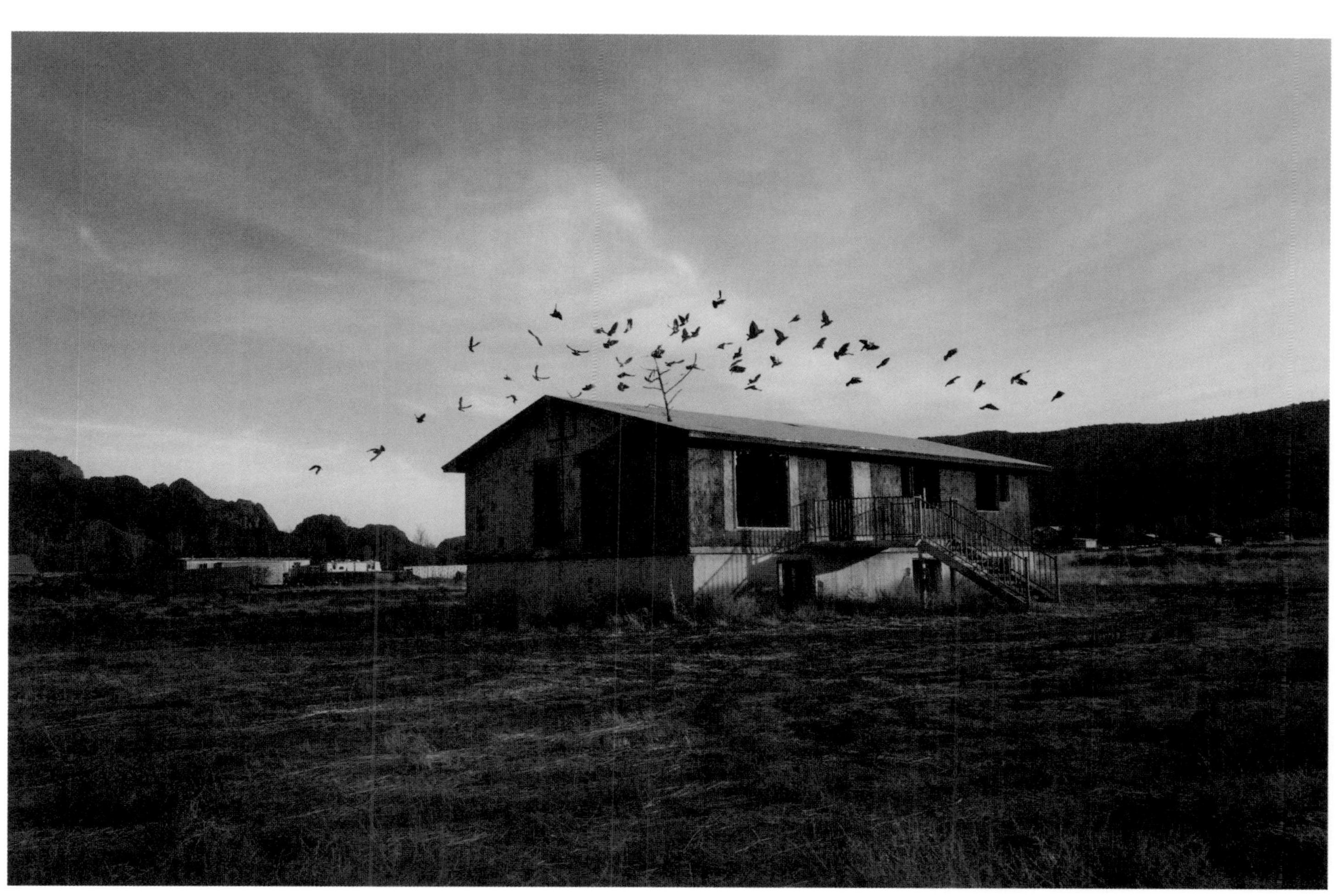

THE CRICK

~ 1 ~

The boys arrive slowly, appearing one by one on horseback over the lip of the ravine, plunging down the steep banks with their mounts sliding on their hocks, or in the case of Ephraim arriving in a truck pulling a long stock trailer full of horses including seven mustangs, a pack horse, and a pony. In the morning light, the horses are unloaded, hooves clattering as they emerge, their pale breath hanging on the cold December air. More boys show up, including Trayl who rides in on a yellow horse leading his "zorse," a cross between a zebra and a horse that he is still training and which he keeps snubbed up close. Most of the horses the boys own are mustangs, hardy animals taken from the open range and rescued from government holding pens. All the mustangs have been freeze-branded on their necks and the white numbers stand out against their dark winter coats like the script of some long forgotten language now no longer decipherable. The boys are dressed in attire from another century, buckskin shirts and vests they have stitched and decorated themselves, wearing hats with stained brims pulled low against the bright sun now shining down upon the boisterous scene. A small brown mustang is saddled for me and we set off in bunches of twos and threes down a sandy path along a stream running low this late in the year.

~ 2 ~

The boys intend to ride down the crick today, the stream that comes out of the mountains to the north and cuts through the small town of Short Creek—or Colorado City, known locally as the Crick—before crossing under the highway where it's channeled into a wide wash with high sandy banks on either side. It's late in the year and the water is low and the same red color as the dirt that surrounds it. When it rains the creek rages and sweeps away all in its path and collects detritus from far away washed down into its channel; it is known for flash floods that can erupt so suddenly anyone caught unaware can perish. Deaths from such things are not uncommon in this country. But the boys are not unaware. They are experienced in all the ways of surviving and navigating this world. They know this slick-rock country, have been raised here in plural families in this town that straddles the Utah-Arizona border, in households with one father and his multiple wives. Some of the boys are related by birth—half-brothers with different mothers and the same father—and some are full brothers or cousins, but whatever their familial connections they have formed a kind of band of brothers and are now bonded irrevocably through their history and their love of horses and of each other, and by their custom of dressing as 19th century explorers, in fringed buckskin shirts and leggings with knives and pistols strapped to their belts and rifle scabbards attached to their saddles, venturing out into the far reaches of this otherworldly landscape where they perform extraordinary feats of horsemanship for their own pleasure and for each other, and in more recent times for the photographer Jim Mangan.

They have taught Jim how to ride. In the beginning they tested his mettle, putting him on a half-broke mustang and cheering him on when he managed to stay in the saddle as the fractious horse reared and threatened to fall upon him. They call him Jimbangin'. He met them when they were still teenagers, some as young as fifteen; the oldest is now twenty-one. He's taken many pictures of them while riding this creek, especially in the place where it widens out into a broad wash, a favorite place for improvising the kinds of feats the boys enjoy, such as plunging off a sheer bluff on a horse and landing on the steep loose scree or skittering up a hard rock outcropping only to stand atop their saddle when they reach the pinnacle.

~ 3 ~

They have ridden together during all seasons, Jim and the boys, on trails winding through the desert near Mesquite and in the mountains and the slot canyons in the surrounding red-rock country where the slick sandstone walls offer passages so narrow and so suffused with rubious light it's like riding through the chambers of a glowing heart. They have ridden into the Canaan Mountains, and the Lost Comanche Trail on Pine Mountain in winter and spent the night in an old abandoned log cabin and the next day cut a path through the deep snow to Big Water Lake and galloped across the frozen ice and then come back to the cabin and lit a fire in the woodstove and sat around a table made from old floor planks where somewhat incongruously the Book of Mormon has been left sitting next to a copy of *High Country News* and pack of Jack Daniels playing cards. The next day descending the trail they can look across the valley dotted with farms at the looming red mountain known as Kolob, or the Seat of God, and below that the snow-covered ridges and broken rock outcroppings stand out white against the slopes of particolored stone upthrust in ragged shelves above the town of Cedar.

~ 4 ~

The town where the boys were raised—the Crick—was ruled by a prophet whose word they were bound to obey until the prophet was convicted of sexually abusing minors and sent to prison in 2011, receiving a life sentence, and then things slowly began to change though the prophet still demanded obeisance from his prison cell. During his final days, as he became more paranoid, he excommunicated many people for their sins—for watching a movie, or listening to music, wearing a short-sleeved shirt or showing interest in a girl. Before that time, before the fall of the prophet, many of the teenage boys were cast out, as had been the custom for many generations. They were left to fend for themselves to ensure the older men had no competition for the younger girls. These boys were referred to as the lost boys only they were not lost they were forsaken, cast beyond the pale to fend for themselves in a world they did not know.

Many of the houses in town are over-sized to accommodate the plural families and have never been finished on the outside because according to the local code if a house hasn't been finished you don't have to pay taxes. The streets are often left unpaved and muddy in spring, and the walls and fences that once encircled family compounds have begun to deteriorate, the metal warped and buckled, the boards now broken into weathered slats and rough slabs lying upon the red earth in various states of decay and everywhere there is the sense of detritus that has been left in some state of abandonment. After the prophet's fall many of his followers fled the Crick. But the boys did not flee. They stayed on, many living with their mothers.

~ 5 ~

The boys ride down the creek in small groups bunched up, a dozen or so kids traveling on mustangs along the wet sand, trailed by five exuberant dogs and two loose ponies. Some of the boys lead pack-horses equipped with the kind of tack required to travel the backcountry where they have camped and ridden since a young age. They turn back and circle each other on their mounts, laughing and playful, and when Jim stops and gets off his horse to take a picture they also stop and wait for him and then call out with mock impatience, "Cowboy up! Let's go!" And to see the jocular and intimate way they treat him is to know he has earned their respect and complete trust and this is not easy to do with these boys who have been raised to distrust outsiders.

When they come to the area where the wash widens into a broad flat plain they dismount and build a fire and we stand around it for a while, warming ourselves against the chill brought on by the fading light and then one after another a few boys mount the unbroken zorse, still snubbed up close by Trayl on his own horse, and they trot and then canter side by side in ever-widening circles around and around, the wind ruffling Trayl's long blonde hair blowing like the fringe on his buckskin jacket. Some of the boys perform feats of agility, standing in the saddle, leaping over their horse's head. They have names that hearken back to patriarchs of old, like Ephraim and Parley, and others, like Laredo, bear a name that evokes a Western movie. Two boys, Chevron and Maverick have rather charmingly been named after gas stations. They were born forty-five minutes apart, to different mothers but the same father, and their bond runs deep; they could be fraternal twins and instead are closest friends, raised side by side and now inseparable. Skylar and Jobee are half brothers, as are Ashley and Jordan. They are among the youngest of the boys, a wild exuberant bunch, and none more so than Jobee, with his superior physical agility and an energy that pours out of him in an endless stream of high spirits. Ephraim, with his calm, wise persona and ability to read a situation, clearly holds a special place in the group, which also includes his brothers Tristan, Callahan, and Ammon—all Barlows and all descended from one of the original founders of Short Creek.

~ 6 ~

Everything is red in this country. Red or orange or mauve or some shade thereof, the rocks and buttes and the scree and scarps and the wind-sculpted pinnacles they call hoodoos which look like human figures wrapped tightly in robes with their featureless heads protruding against the sky, everything all red in this land, the color of rust or dried blood. The sheer stone walls of the tall mountains forming a backdrop to the Crick are lit by the setting sun as I ride back with the boys six hours later, to the place where we began, and the curtain of red cliffs looks illuminated from within like fire rocks burning in the sunset. Many of the houses in town once had badges near the front door that said "Zion," announcing their owner's belief in this place as the anointed land chosen by God for his favored people. The Zion badges are now mostly gone, another sign of the prophet's fall, but the belief in the world of flaming rocks has not faded. Some evenings it's said spirits manifest themselves in these rocks, emerging from the stones and the shadows and in the light falling upon the face of the cliffs one can see the face of Jesus and the prophets of old, or the shapes and forms of wingless angels and floating heads. Such is the power of the land depicted in these photographs, with the lightning-struck pines and truncated stumps and the rivers running red, where the whorls of rock and the whorls of stone and water and trees cast a furious, surging beauty. That is what Jim Mangan has captured in these pictures of both the changing boys and their changing world.

—Judith Freeman, February 27, 2022

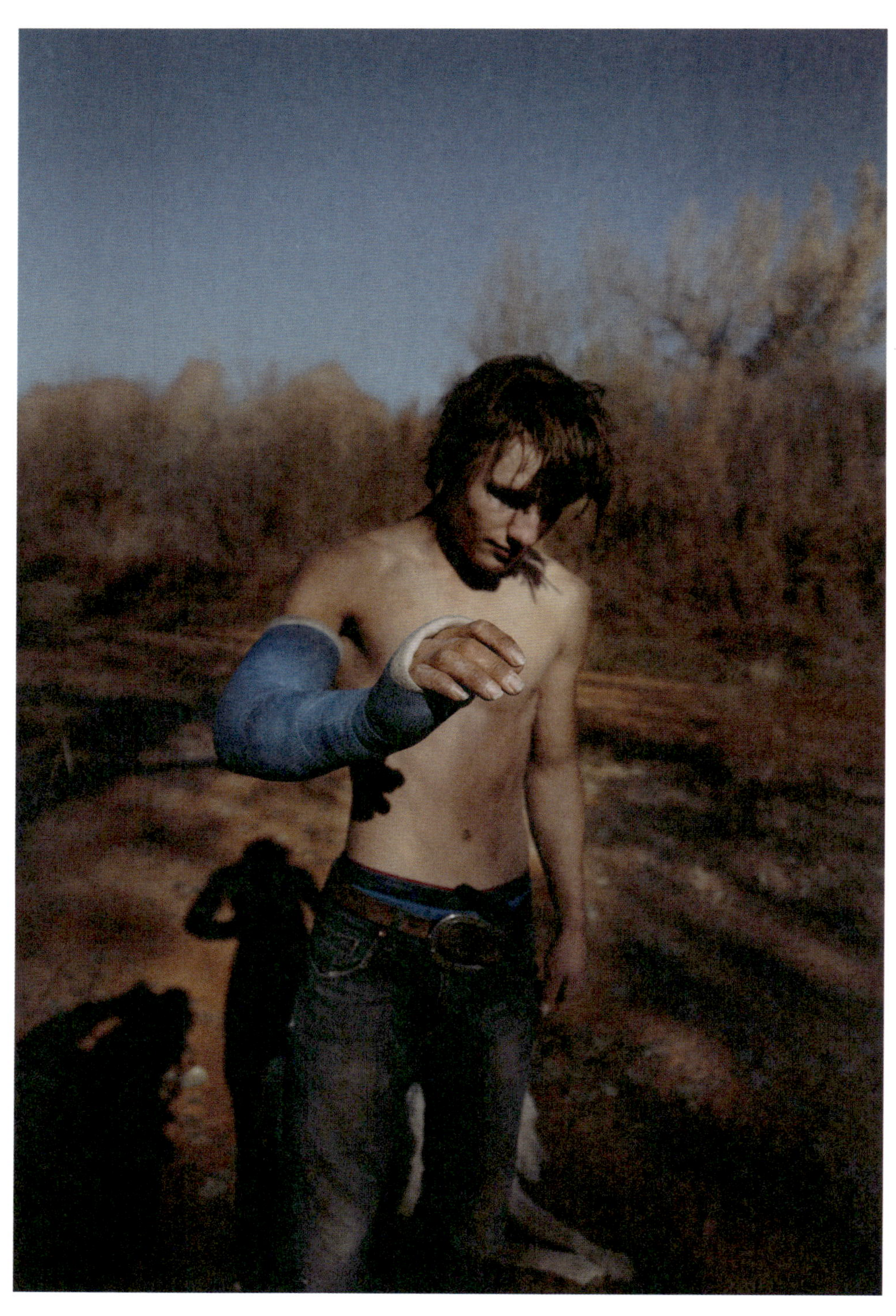

ACKNOWLEDGMENTS

This project would not have been possible without the featured men and boys, to whom I am eternally grateful—

Ephriam Barlow
Jobee Cooke
Trayl Jessop
Chevron Barlow
Tyson Cooke
Ashley Cooke
Tristan Barlow
Milan Cooke
Callahan Barlow
Maverick Barlow
Jordan Cooke
Alexander Dutson
Laredo Barlow
Parley Stubbs
Mark Roundy
Skyler Cooke
Howard Barlow
Ammon Barlow

Special thanks to the following folks—

Jenny Le, Sherry Mangan Fascetta, Jim Mangan Sr, Ross Fascetta, Carrie Hess, Mike Hess, Penelope Steiner, Cynthia Combs, Tiffany Howorka, Jim and Janet Van Huysse, Roman Bateman, Kevin Messina, Jack Woody, Judith Freeman, Bryan Schutmaat, Matthew Genitempo, Trevor Parlo Clement, Lee Friedlander, Richard Avedon, Tucker Phillips, Erynn Patrick Lamont, Will Doyle, Kenzie Dutson, Ty Cooke, LeAnna and Willy Cooke, Johna Meldrum, William Ephriam Barlow Sr., Alie Meldrum, Dee Jessop, Nich McElroy, Terry Soo Park, Jackie Bates, Jessie Wender, Justin Guthrie, Justin Suazo, Mark Bauch, Peter MacGill, Maia Ruth Lee, Peter Sutherland, Heyward Hart, Michelle Le, Torbjørn Rødland, Ari Marcopoulos, Mahmoud 'Mo' Mfinanga, Jordan Sullivan, Coley Brown, Sara Hantman, Clint Woodside, David Strettell, Cole Barash, Joe Leavenworth, Light Work, Thomas Line, Dan Boardman, Whitney Hubbs, Cjala Surratt, Rebecca Marris, Ryan Krueger, Victor Rivera, Julie Herman, Elissa Wall, Tina Barney, Norma Jean Markus, Carol Körting, Morgan Crowcroft-Brown.

THE CRICK

Jim Mangan

Available worldwide through D.A.P. | Distributed Art Publishers
75 Broad Street, Suite 630, New York, New York 10004 ~ www.artbook.com

ISBN 978-1-936611-22-5

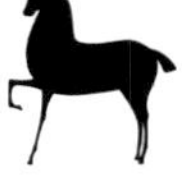

TWIN PALMS PUBLISHERS

Los Angeles, California ~ www.twinpalms.com

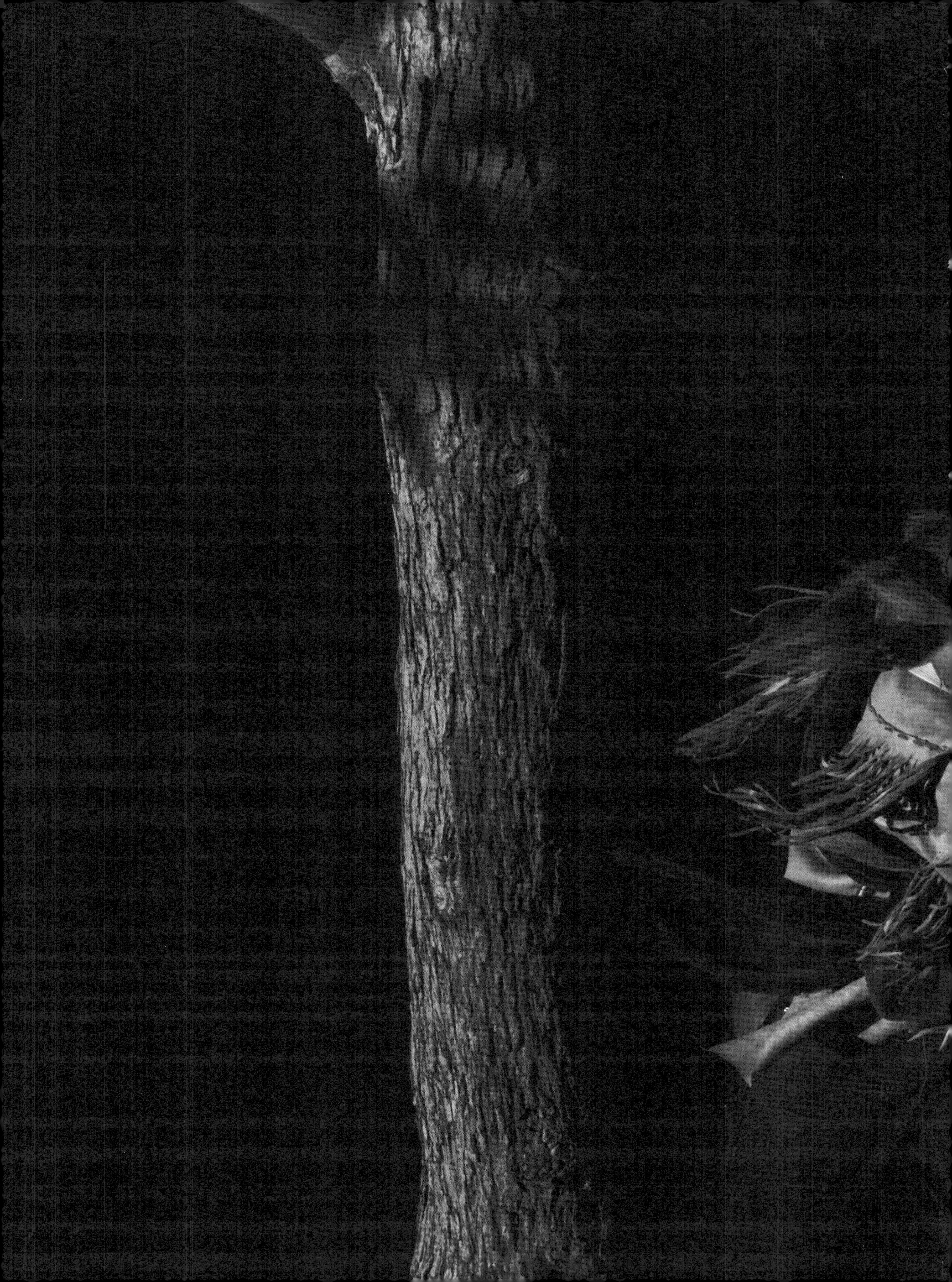